STARTING OUT!®
Workbook

Building Essential Life Skills

To be used with *Starting Out!*® book plus companion website, www.startingout.com
User log-in: WB8407

Education

Bothell, WA • Chicago, IL • Columbus, OH • New York, NY

www.mheonline.com

 **Education**

Send all inquiries to:
McGraw-Hill Education
130 East Randolph Street, Suite 400
Chicago, IL 60601

ISBN: 978-0-07-660759-4
MHID: 0-07-660759-3

Printed in the United States of America.

5 6 7 8 9 QDB 15 14 13 12 11

The **McGraw·Hill** Companies

Table of Contents

Preface
Welcome to the Starting Out!® Workbook

Applying Life Skills to Real-life Decisions

This workbook has been developed for students, recent graduates, job program participants, and those transitioning out of the Armed Forces. It is designed to be used with the Starting Out!® handbook.

Life often presents complicated and at times difficult decisions, such as how to evaluate personal skills and interests, how to find the best career training program, where to find financial aid for further education, whether or not to move out of the family home, or how to address health or family problems.

To become good decision makers when facing these and other challenges, we need to build practical, core skills, known as "life skills," just as we build academic and occupational skills while in school.

The first part of this book, entitled "Understanding and Mastering Life's Core Skills," defines important life skills. These life skills are being presented for discussion purposes, so that the reader can be aware of the strategies and techniques for dealing effectively with interpersonal relationships, life problems and conflicts, and career and family decisions.

The remainder of the book presents thirty real-life situations that require the application of these life skills in order to make sound decisions. We have tried to depict these thirty chapters in an engaging, practical, and informative way.

As you tackle each interactive chapter, you will be building important life management skills that will come in handy over and over as you go through life.

Good luck with your journey!

Introduction:
Understanding and Mastering Life's Core Skills

Adapted from Educational Materials Developed by UNICEF and the World Health Organization

I. What are Life Skills?

The World Health Organization defines life skills as "the abilities for adaptive and positive behavior that enable individuals to deal effectively with the demands and challenges of everyday life."

Similarly, UNICEF, a United Nations organization, defines life skills as "a behavior change or behavior development approach designed to address a balance of three areas: knowledge, attitude and skills." The UNICEF definition is based on research evidence that suggests that shifts in behavior are unlikely if knowledge, attitudinal, and skills-based competency are not addressed.

Life skills are essentially those abilities that help promote mental well-being and competence in people as they face the realities of life. Most development professionals agree that life skills are generally applied in the context of health and social events. However, they can be utilized in many areas, such as: prevention of drug use, sexual violence, teenage pregnancy, HIV/AIDS prevention, and suicide prevention.

Life skills can also extends into consumer education, environmental education, peace education or education for development, livelihood and income generation, among others.

In short, life skills empower people to take positive action.

II. What are the Core Life Skill Strategies and Techniques?

UNICEF (United Nations International Children's Emergency Fund), UNESCO (United National Educational, Social and Cultural Organization), and WHO (World Health Organization) list the core life skill strategies and techniques as:

1. **Problem Solving**
2. **Critical Thinking**
3. **Effective Communication Skills**
4. **Decision Making**
5. **Interpersonal Relationship Skills**
6. **Self-Awareness Building Skills**
7. **Empathy**
8. **Coping with stress and emotions**

Self-awareness, self-esteem and self-confidence are essential tools for understanding one's strengths and weaknesses. Consequently, the individual is able to discern available opportunities and prepare to face possible problems. This mindset leads to the development of a social awareness of the concerns of one's family and society. Subsequently, it is possible to identify and address problems that arise within both the family and society.

With life skills, one is able to explore alternatives, weigh pros and cons, and make rational decisions to solve each problem or issue as it arises. It also entails being able to establish productive interpersonal relationships with others.

III. What are the Main Components of Life Skills?

The World Health Organization categorizes life skills into the following three components:

1) Communication/Interpersonal Skills include verbal and non-verbal communication, active listening, and the ability to express feelings and give feedback. Also in this category are negotiation/refusal skills and assertiveness skills that directly affect one's ability to manage conflict. Empathy, which is the ability to listen and understand others' needs, is also a key interpersonal skill. Teamwork and the ability to cooperate are skills that include expressing respect for those around us. Development of this skill set enables one to be accepted in society. These skills result in the acceptance of social norms that provide the foundation for adult social behavior.

2) Decision Making / Critical Thinking Skills include decision making/problem solving skills and information gathering skills. The individual must also be skilled at evaluating the future consequences of his or her present actions and the actions of others. One needs to be able to determine alternative solutions and to analyze the influence of one's own values and the values of those around him or her.

3) Coping and Self-Management Skills refers to skills that increase the internal locus of control, so that the individual believes that he or she can make a difference in the world and affect change. Self-esteem, self-awareness, self-evaluation skills and the ability to set goals are also part of the more general category of self-management skills. Anger, grief, and anxiety must all be dealt with, and the individual learns to cope with loss or trauma. Stress management and time management are equally important, as are positive thinking and relaxation techniques.

Here is a convenient outline summary, by category, of these life skills:

Communication and Interpersonal Skills

Interpersonal communication skills
Verbal/Nonverbal communication
Active listening
Expressing feelings; giving feedback (without blaming) and receiving feedback

Negotiation/refusal skills
Negotiation and conflict management
Assertiveness skills
Refusal skills

Empathy

Ability to listen and understand another's needs and circumstances and express that understanding

Cooperation and Teamwork

Expressing respect for others' contributions and different styles
Assessing one's own abilities and contributing to the group

Decision Making and Critical Thinking Skills

Decision making / problem solving skills

Information gathering skills
Evaluating future consequences of present actions for self and others
Determining alternative solutions to problems
Analysis skills regarding the influence of values and attitudes of self and others on motivation

Critical thinking skills

Analyzing peer and media influences
Analyzing attitudes, values, social norms and beliefs and factors affecting these
Identifying relevant information and information sources

Coping and Self-Management Skills

Skills for increasing internal locus of control

Self esteem/confidence building skills
Self awareness skills including awareness of rights, influences, values, attitudes, strengths and weaknesses
Goal setting skills
Self evaluation / Self assessment / Self-monitoring skills

Skills for managing feelings

Anger management
Dealing with grief and anxiety
Coping skills for dealing with loss, abuse, trauma

Skills for managing stress

Time management
Positive thinking
Relaxation techniques

IV: Using this Workbook

This Workbook should be fun to read, and informative for anybody who takes the time to delve into each scenario and find the best solutions. The primary resource to consult is your copy of the *Starting Out!®* handbook, *along with resources at the end of the workbook chapters and your favorite Internet search engine. This workbook can help develop your research skill to obtain practical information that will enhance your life skills. You can repeatedly use the completed worksheets as a resource when applicable situations arise in the future.*

Even if you are not yet apt to face some of the issues in this Workbook, they have been carefully selected as situations that are bound to arise, sooner or later, so you will be well-prepared to handle them in a smart way when they come along!

Good luck, and have fun on the life journey you are about to take through this new book.

Chapter 1

Finding a Route to a Good Job

You're tired of low-paying jobs and living paycheck to paycheck. Perhaps you are ready for some serious job training. What are your options?

Goals:

1) Learn about different ways to get job training.
2) Learn about pairing occupations with training.
3) Learn about financial aid for occupational training.
4) Learn about different levels of education and corresponding pay scales.

Use Part II of Starting Out!® and your own Internet research to complete the following.

While it's not impossible to earn a good living with little education, there is definitely a correlation between education and earnings. Besides pay, what are two other benefits of job training and education?

1) _____

2) _____

Does it sometimes feel like college is the only place to get job training and education? There are actually quite a few options, depending on your interests and career goals. Compare the following job training programs or facilities:

Type of Program/School	Length of Program	Cost of Program	2-3 Examples of Training Fields
Community College			
Career and Vocational Schools			
Apprenticeships			

Distance Education			
Government-Sponsored Adult Training Programs			

It is possible to decide on the type of program you like, and choose an occupation based on what it offers. However, you can also decide on an occupation you're interested in, and then find out what type of training you'd need to pursue it. Using Chapter 8 of Starting Out!®, the *Occupational Outlook Handbook* online (www.bls.gov/oco/), and your own research, write down two jobs you're interested in and the type of training they require:

Job 1:	Training:
Job 2:	Training:

Perhaps you're concerned about the cost of an educational or job training program. Fortunately, there are many different funding sources out there. Use chapter 11 of the Starting Out!® handbook to define the four basic types of financial aid:

Grants: _____

_____

Scholarships: _____

_____

Loans: _____

_____

Work Study: _____

_____

When trying to decide on a program, be sure to ask about financial assistance at each school's admissions office.

 **Resources**

CareerOneStop: Training and Education Center
http://www.careeronestop.org/training/trainingEduHome.asp
CareerOneStop, operated by the U.S. Department of Labor with field locations in every state, offers excellent resources and assistance to individuals seeking career training. At this comprehensive site you can assess your abilities and locate training programs.

Chapter 2

How to Afford a 4-Year College Education

Y ou would really like to go to a community or four-year college, but you're worried you can't afford it. You've heard about scholarships before, but how can you learn more? Are there any other options to help make college more affordable?

Goals:
1) Learn about the differences between community, public, and private colleges and universities.
2) Learn about the different types of financial aid (grants, loans, scholarships, and work study).
3) Locate scholarships that could apply to you.

Use Part II of Starting Out!®, the resources in this chapter, and your own Internet research to complete the following.

Many people start their higher education at a community or two-year college, and then transfer to a university for their final two years. Community colleges are usually less expensive than a private or even public four-year institution. Where is the nearest community college to you? (Use this community college finder from the American Association of Community Colleges: www.aacc.nche.edu/Pages/CCFinder.aspx.)

_____

Which programs sound interesting to you?
_____
_____
_____

Grants, loans, scholarships, and work study programs (discussed in Chapter 1) can help offset the cost of a college education, and can be found on a national, state, and local level. Locate a potential national source of financial aid and write the name of it and the potential award below:

_____
_____

Now do the same for a source of funding from your state:

_____
_____

Finally, find three non-governmental scholarships that may be applicable to you and fill in the table below. You can use a scholarship search engine, use a resource from Chapter 11 of Starting Out!®, or do a search for "state scholarships" in a standard search engine.

Name	Eligibility Requirements	Reward

 **Resources**

Federal Student Aid Resources

http://studentaid.ed.gov

The U.S. Department of Education operates this website to provide students with assistance in locating financial aid. It has extensive resources to help you find scholarships, student loans, and other financial assistance.

State Financial Aid

http://www.students.gov

Planning and paying for your education are the key themes at this federal government website. Click on the link called Pay for Your Education and visit individual state-by-state web resources.

College Board: Scholarship Search

http://apps.collegeboard.com/cbsearch_ss/welcome.jsp

The College Board offers a powerful search engine to find scholarships from a variety of sources. There are also financial aid planning tools, resources on student loans, as well as family tax benefits for tuition payments.

Chapter 3

Evaluating Interests, Skills, and Related Jobs

You've graduated from high school, and everyone keeps asking, "So, what kind of job do you want to get?" The problem is, you don't know. You've excelled at certain classes, have experience and skills in certain areas, and have lots of interests. How can you combine all these things to find the job that's right for you?

Goals:

1) Assess your interests, skills, and experience.
2) Learn about occupations and training.

Use Chapter 12 and 13 of Starting Out!®, the resources in this chapter, and your own Internet research to complete the charts that follow.

One way to figure out which career path to follow is to do a self-assessment. Doing one gets you to think about your skills, interests, and experience, and also about the kind of work environment you'd prefer. The following activities will get you started.

First, think about your skills.

✓ **Check all that apply**

☐	I am a good writer.	☐	I am good at building things.
☐	I am creative.	☐	I am very organized.
☐	I am outgoing and enjoy helping others.	☐	I am skilled at using computer software and/or computer programming.
☐	I work well with animals.	☐	I am athletic.
☐	I am good at math.	☐	I am a good leader and can supervise others.
☐	I do well in science .	☐	I have good debate skills.

Think about your interests.

✓ **Check all that apply**

☐	I like to cook.	☐	I like working with plants.
☐	I like to perform lab experiments and/or use a microscope.	☐	I am interested in learning/discovering new things.
☐	I like building or repairing things and working with tools.	☐	I am interested in writing or journalism.
☐	I like teaching people.	☐	I am interested in politics and economics.
☐	I like to paint, sculpt, or create other artwork.	☐	I am interested in helping sick or injured people.
☐	I enjoy research and problem solving.	☐	I am interested in news and politics.

How do you feel about different work environments?

✓ **Check all that apply**

☐	I like to work independently.	☐	I like to work on the computer.
☐	I like to work with other people.	☐	I like working with tools or machines.
☐	I like working with children.	☐	I like working outdoors.
☐	I like to follow a routine.	☐	I like working from home.
☐	I like doing a variety of tasks.	☐	I like working in a laboratory or technical facility.
☐	I like to follow precisely defined procedures.	☐	I like a relatively quiet work environment.
☐	I like to express myself creatively.	☐	I like a fast-paced work environment.

Finally, using one of the sites listed in the Resources section, take an online assessment using some of your answers from above. What careers did it suggest for you?

1) _____

2) _____

3) _____

4) _____

Pick the top two careers you may be interested in pursuing. Use the Internet and Chapters 8 and 9 of Starting Out® to find out what type of training and education you would need for them.

Career		Suggested education/training	
Career		Suggested education/training	

 **Resources**

Ability, Interest, & Career Assessment Tools
iSeek: Skills Assessment
http://www.iseek.org/careers/skillsAssessment

Examine your skills and values with the iSeek Skills Assessment to learn about future career directions. You can also learn more about how your interests can lead to a certain occupational field by using the MnCareers Interest Assessment..

Department of Labor Commission on Achieving Necessary Skills
http://www.soicc.state.nc.us/SOICC/planning/skillsjob.htm

The Commission on Achieving Necessary Skills within the U.S. Department of Labor developed two groups of important workplace skills: foundation skills and functional skills, as described on this website.

Career Information
Occupational Outlook Handbook
http://www.bls.gov/oco/home.htm

For hundreds of different types of jobs, such as teacher, painter, and plumber, the *Occupational Outlook Handbook* describes (a) the training and education needed, (b) earnings, (c) job prospects, (d) what workers do on the job, and (e) working conditions.

Bureau of Labor Statistics: What do You Like?
http://www.bls.gov/k12

Based on your current interests, this website suggests occupations that you might consider. For each suggested occupation, there is a full profile describing the nature of the career.

Chapter 4

Preparing a Resume and Searching for Jobs

With some occupations in mind, you're ready to check out employers and look for a job. You know you need to create a resume, and you would also like to find some information on interviewing skills. Also, you want to know where the best places are to find out about jobs that are available.

Goals:

1) Create a resume.
2) Learn about writing a cover letter.
3) Learn about interview skills.
4) Learn where to find job postings.
5) Learn about career help on the web.

Use Chapters 14 through 16 of Starting Out!® and your own Internet research to complete the following activities.

Step One:

First you need to find a job for which you'd like to apply. In chapter 15 of Starting Out!®, you'll find a number of different job search engines listed. Choose one, and do a practice job search. Enter your preferred location and a category or a keyword, and write down three jobs that you find interesting.

Search Engine: _____ Location:_____ Category/Keyword:_____

	1	2	3
Jobs Found:			

Step Two:

Almost all companies and state and local governments have their own job pages. Do an Internet search and find the job page of two companies, organizations, or government agencies that you are interested in. Write the web addresses below:

1) _____

2) _____

Step Three: Preparing a Resume

Now you need to create a resume. Remember, a resume can be useful for a number of jobs, or you can tailor it to a specific job. Review the sample resumes in Chapter 14 of Starting Out!™ and think about and gather information about your talents, experiences, employment history, and education. Also think about the clubs and organizations you belong to and any special skills or certifications you may have, such as a driver's license or a first aid certification. Then use the following template to create your resume:

Your Name:
Address:
City, State Zip Code:

Phone Number:
e-mail:

OBJECTIVE: This describes your employment goal.

EDUCATION
Type of Diploma, Certificate, or Degree (attained or expected):
Focus of study (GPA optional):
School Name, City, State:

SUMMARY OF QUALIFICATIONS: Short summary of skills, accomplishments, or responsibilities related to this specific job.

Qualification 1:

Qualification 2:

Qualification 3:

SUMMARY OF EXPERIENCE: Job, volunteer, special program

Title:
Employer: City, State: Dates:
Duties:

Title:
Employer: City, State: Dates:
Duties:

LICENSES AND CERTIFICATIONS

MEMBERSHIP IN ORGANIZATIONS

AWARDS OR RECOGNITION

REFERENCES
Name: Phone number:

Name: Phone number:

Step Four: Writing a Cover Letter

When applying for a job, you will almost always want to include a cover letter with your resume. A cover letter lets the employer know a little bit more about you, including why you are interested in their job and why you would be the perfect candidate. Using the sample cover letter in Chapter 14 of Starting Out!®, Internet resources, and the following template, write a practice cover letter for your dream job:

Your Name
Street Address
City, State   Zip Code
Phone Number

Date

Individual's Name
Job Title
Name of Organization
Street Address
City, State Zip Code

Dear Mr. / Ms.

First Paragraph: State the reason for writing. Name the specific position or type of work for which you're applying. Mention how you learned of the opening.

Second Paragraph: Explain why you're interested in working for this employer and specify how you're PERFECT for this position. Don't repeat the information on your resume, but instead include something special or unique about yourself that will benefit the employer. Also remember that the reader will consider this an example of your writing skills.

Third Paragraph: Mention that your resume is enclosed and indicate your desire to meet with the employer. You may want to suggest alternate dates and times, or simply advise them of your flexibility to the time and place.

Include day and evening contact information. Include a statement or question that will encourage the reader to respond. Be sure to communicate your plan to follow up. You might state that you'll be in the area on a certain date and would like to set up a meeting, or you'll call on a certain date to set up a meeting. Finally, thank the employer for his/her time.
Sincerely,

(Your Signature in blue or black ink)
Your typed name

Enclosure (such as your resume and copies of transcripts or certifications)

Step Five: The Job Interview

Hopefully, your cover letter and resume will bring you to the next step in the job hunt: an interview.

Interview preparation is very important. One key thing to do is to learn more about the employer and the specific job or type of job before you arrive at the interview, so you can speak knowledgably and better convey why you'd like to work there. Review the company's website. You can also use this information to ask more in-depth questions. What are two questions you would ask your ideal employer?

1) _____

2) _____

What are 3 common interview questions that you might be asked? How would you answer them?

Question	Answer
Example: What are your greatest strengths?	Example: I am able to work on muliple projects at the same time while still meeting dealines.

What are some other general tips for having a successful interview? List three things you can do to give the best impression. (Example: Upon meeting the interviewer, thank him or her for taking the time to meet with you.)

1) _____

2) _____

3) _____

Chapter 5

Your First Paycheck: Why So Many Deductions?

Y ou just received your paycheck... Why does it look so small? When you were hired, you were told you'd be getting $10/hour for a 40-hour work week. 10 times 40 is $400... How come your paycheck is less than this? Where did all the money go?

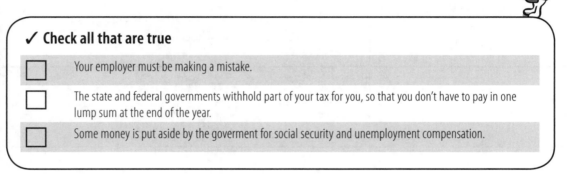

✓ **Check all that are true**

☐ Your employer must be making a mistake.

☐ The state and federal governments withhold part of your tax for you, so that you don't have to pay in one lump sum at the end of the year.

☐ Some money is put aside by the goverment for social security and unemployment compensation.

Goals:

1) learn about required payroll deductions.
2) Learn about voluntary deductions.
3) Learn about unemployment insurance and disability.
4) Learn why under-the-table jobs are not worth taking.

Use Chapter 20 of Starting Out!® and your own Internet research to complete the following.

Please define the following types of deductions...

Federal Income Tax:

_____

_____

Social Security:

_____

_____

Medicare:

_____

_____

State Income Tax:

_____

_____

Unemployment and Disability Insurance:

_____

_____

There are some types of deductions that are voluntary. Usually these are programs that are offered through your employer, such as health insurance, that you can opt for or not. What is another voluntary deduction?

_____

_____

Someone offers to pay you for your work "under-the-table"—in other words, in cash—so there won't be any deductions. Is this a good idea? What are some of the pros and cons?

_____

_____

_____

What are some of the consequences of not claiming some of your income?

_____

_____

_____

_____

 **Resources**

Payroll Deductions Calculator
http:///www.bankrate.com/calculators/tax-planning/payroll-tax-deductions-calculator.aspx
This site features a calculator to help you figure out how deductions change take-home pay. Definitions of terms related to payroll deductions are also provided.

Cash Course: Reviewing Paycheck Deductions
http://www.cashcourse.org/snc/Article.aspx?218
This brief article describes the four basic paycheck tax deductions.

Chapter 6

Employment Rights: Keeping the Workplace Fair

Your boss often expects you to work a lot more than 40 hours per week. This doesn't seem fair, but you are afraid to raise any questions. Your friends and family tell you that he can't make you work so much, but you don't want to lose this job. What can you do?

Goals:

1) Learn about employment rights and wage and hour laws.
2) Learn about job discrimination.
3) Learn about reporting a problem and retaliation.

Use Chapter 17 of Starting Out!®, the resources in this chapter, and your own Internet research to complete the following.

In the United States, there are a number of state and federal laws that protect employee rights, which include the right to a safe work environment and freedom from discrimination, harassment, unfair treatment, and retaliation. If you believe you are being treated unfairly by your employer, you can check state and federal laws to find out what you can do.

Locate your state's labor law website, and write its address below:

_____

It is not illegal for your boss to have you work more than 40 hours a week. However, it is illegal for him or her not to pay you overtime pay for any hours beyond 40, unless you are an "exempt" employee. What is the overtime rate in your state?

_____

_____

What types of employees are considered "exempt" relative to extra overtime pay?

_____

_____

Circle one: You should be told **before** or **after** you are hired whether you are classified as an exempt employee.

What is your state's minimum wage?

_____

What is the federal minimum wage?

_____

Workplace harassment and discrimination are outlawed by state and federal laws. Harassment involves being bothered, distressed, or tormented persistently. What types of actions qualify as harassment?

_____

_____

How do you file a harassment complaint in your state?

_____

_____

Discrimination means being treated differently based on prejudice against a class or category. Give two examples of discrimination.

    1) _____

    2) _____

If a discrimination claim persists after you speak with your employer, you can file a claim through a state agency or through the federal Equal Employment Opportunity Commission. How do you file a complaint in your state?

_____

_____

Employers can sometimes react negatively to having a charge filed against them. What is retaliation?

_____

_____

What can you do if you suspect retaliation?

_____

_____

While some occupations involve certain hazards, your workplace is required by law to be as safe as possible. The Occupational Safety and Health Administration (OSHA) creates safe workplace standards and works to see that they are enforced. On its website (see "Resources"), you can find standards for different occupations and working conditions as well as how-to guides to protect yourself in different conditions, including what types of personal protective equipment should be used.

What should you do if you feel your employer is allowing an unsafe work environment to exist?

_____

_____

_____

_____

Resources

Fair Labor Standards Act
http://www.dol.gov/compliance/laws/comp-flsa.htm

Read all about the Fair Labor Standards Act, the core legislation that established the minimum wage, standard working hours, overtime pay, and protections against child labor.

Equal Employment Opportunity Commission
http://www.eeoc.gov

The EEOC enforces laws protecting employees against discrimination based upon race, color, religion, sex, and national origin. There are also laws against sex-based discrimination, age discrimination, and discrimination against those who are disabled. The Civil Rights Act of 1991 enacted monetary damages in discrimination cases.

Workplace Fairness: Resources
http://www.workplacefairness.org/resources

Find information on this website about workplace fairness issues and how they are handled in each state, as well as by industry, subject, and worker type.

U.S. Department of Justice: Upholding Civil Rights and Liberties
http://www.usdoj.gov/crt/

Established in 1957, the Civil Rights Division of the Department of Justice is the principal government agency responsible for enforcing federal laws prohibiting discrimination on the basis of race, sex, disability, religion, and national origin. Learn how to file a federal discrimination complaint regarding disabilities, educational opportunities, employment, housing, and voting.

Occupational Safety and Health Administration
http://www.osha.gov

Under the Occupational Safety and Health Act of 1970, employers are responsible for providing a safe and healthy workplace for their employees. OSHA's role is to promote the safety and health of America's working men and women by setting and enforcing standards; providing training, outreach, and education; establishing partnerships; and encouraging continual process improvement in workplace safety and health.

Chapter 7

Work Accidents and Workers' Compensation

You are at work when you stumble on the stairs, fall, and break your leg. You can't put weight on it for several weeks and so you can't work while your leg is healing. You don't have enough sick time to cover this accident. Will you still get paid?

Goals:

1) Learn about Workers' Compensation.
2) Learn about federal benefits.
3) Learn about your state's benefits.
4) Learn about employer obligations.

Use Chapter 22 of Starting Out!®, the resources in this chapter, and your own Internet research to complete the following.

State and federal governments have Workers' Compensation Insurance to help you out in this type of situation. What is Workers' Compensation Insurance?

_____
_____
_____

What are two examples of a work-related injury or occupational disease?

1) _____

2) _____

Most workers' compensation falls under the jurisdiction of the states, and so each state has its own workers' compensation board. Locate the web address of your state's workers' compensation board and write it below.

_____

Are the employers in your state required to have workers' compensation insurance?

_____

What types of worker's compensation benefits are available in your state?

     1) _____

     2) _____

     3) _____

In your state, is there a time limit for filing a claim?

_____

What are the employers' obligations in your state, regarding workers' compensation?

_____
_____
_____

What do you do if your employer challenges your workers' compensation claim?

_____
_____
_____
_____

 **Resources**

U.S. Department of Labor: Federal Workers' Compensation

http://www.dol.gov/dol/topic/workcomp/

Information on federal workers' compensation, which applies to federal government employees, can be found at this Department of Labor website.

U.S. Department of Labor: Finding State Workers' Compensation Programs

http://www.dol.gov/esa/owcp/dfec/regs/compliance/wc.htm

Most employees across America are covered by the workers' compensation laws in their own state. This website provides links to each state office of workers' compensation. You can also search for the workers' compensation program in your state using any search engine.

Chapter 8

Why You Need a Personal Budget

Money seems to be going out faster than it's coming in. Gas prices are high, and food prices are going up. How can you keep costs down?

✓ **Check off ideas you would consider to save money:**

- ☐ Make gifts for people instead of buying them.
- ☐ Get books and DVDs from the library.
- ☐ Make your own lunch, instead of buying it.
- ☐ Bring a shopping list to the store, and stick to it.
- ☐ Cook dinner more often instead of going out.
- ☐ Turn off the lights when you leave the room.
- ☐ Stop buying cigarettes.
- ☐ Cut down on entertainment expenses.

Goals:

1) Learn how to create a personal budget.
2) Compare cooking a meal vs. eating out.
3) Compare car use to carpooling or public transportation.
4) Learn how to save money through energy efficiency.
5) Explore other ways to save money.

Use Chapter 30 of Starting Out!®, the resources in this chapter, and your own Internet research to complete the following.

The first place to start when you feel like your spending is getting out of control is to take a close look at what you're earning and what you're spending. Read this example:

- You earn $1500 a month (after taxes) from your primary job, and you have a part-time job that earns you an extra $200.
- Your share of the rent is $400/month. Your share of the basic utilities (electricity, water, and heat) is $50/month.
- Your cell phone service is $50/month, and your share of the cable and is $25/month.
- You charge assorted things, like clothes and CDs, to your credit card, usually between $50 to $100 per month.
- You currently owe $450 on your credit card, and you pay $50/month to pay this off.
- You spend $40/week on groceries, and $60/week on eating out.
- Your car payments are $200/month, and car insurance is $50/month.
- You drive to work, and fill up your tank about once a week, which costs you $40 each time.
- Your share of your health insurance is $75/month.
- You spend about $100/month on additional entertainment.

Wow, no wonder you're feeling like things are tight. They are! You are barely breaking even and have nothing left over for emergencies. You need to create a budget and get things under control. A budget is a list of your income and expenses, used to create a plan and keep your spending under control. Fill in this sample budget with spending shown above (assume four weeks to a month) and a future spending plan:

Category	Current Monthly	Future Monthly
Income:		
Income #1		
Income #2		
Total Income		
Expenses:		
Rent		
Basic utilities		
Phone		
Cable and Internet		
Car expenses		
Health insurance		
Food		
Debt repayment		
Entertainment/ recreation		
Total Expenses		
Income - Expenses =		

If you were stumped on how to reduce your monthly spending, let's take a closer look at a couple of areas.

Food:
How does the cost of eating out compare with cooking at home? Answer this question by noting food prices at your supermarket. Price out the cost of two typical meals (remember: store-bought ingredients can sometimes be used for several meals) and write down your results.

Meal 1: _____
Cost of eating out: _____
Cost of ingredients: _____ + _____ + _____ + _____ = _____

Meal 2: _____
Cost of eating out: _____
Cost of ingredients: _____ + _____ + _____ + _____ = _____

Look online to find three other tips for saving money on food.

1) _____

2) _____

3) _____

Transportation:
If you have to drive to your job, what are two things you can do to improve your gas mileage (without buying a new car)?

1) _____

2) _____

How much would it cost per month to take public transportation? _____

Energy:
Another important way to save money is through energy efficiency. Do some research on the Internet, and find one way to reduce your electric and heating bills.

Save on electricity by:
Save on heat by:

Other:

There are many online resources to help you save money. Find three more ways that you could start spending less money tomorrow:

1) _____

2) _____

3) _____

Now that you've learned more about budgeting, review the budget sheet you filled out earlier, if necessary.

 **Resources**

Budgeting

Money Smart: A Financial Education Program

http://www.fdic.gov/consumers/consumer/moneysmart/overview.html

The Federal Deposit Insurance Corporation (FDIC) has created Money Smart, a training program to help adults outside the financial mainstream enhance their money skills and create positive banking relationships. There are ten program modules, covering such topics as banking, borrowing, saving, safety, credit cards, and home ownership.

Budget Calculator for Students

http://www.ed.gov/offices/OSFAP/DirectLoan/BudgetCalc/budget.html

The Federal Student Aid site of the U.S. Department of Education offers this online program about personal budgeting. You can build your own budget by filling in sources of income and each type of living expense, and then assess whether to make changes to balance income with expenses.

Food

All Things Frugal: Saving Money on Food

http://www.allthingsfrugal.com/foodsave.htm

This convenient and useful site offers numerous ways to save money on groceries, and provides tips for saving in many other budget areas. There is a list of inexpensive but healthy foods, information on where to find food bargains, and recipes for good meals at low prices.

Grocery Saving Tips from CoolSavings.com

http://www.coolsavings.com/grocerytips.aspx

This site includes numerous links offering ways to save on groceries. The grocery-saving section of CoolSavings.com has many good ideas, including ways to obtain and use coupons that are available online.

Transportation

66 Ways to Save Money: Transportation

http://pueblo.gsa.gov/cic_text/money/66ways/content#transportation

Visit this page to find 66 ways to save money on transportation. This includes air fares, car purchases, car repairs, and gasoline.

The Drive Smarter Challenge: Money Saving Tips

http://drivesmarterchallenge.org/money-saving-tips/Default.aspx

The Drive Smarter Challenge website has tips for saving money on transportation. This includes vehicle maintenance tips, tips on using public transportation, and driving tips such as curbing road rage and cleaning out your trunk.

Energy Efficiency

EnergySavers.gov

http://www.energysavers.gov/

This site provides consumers with free and inexpensive strategies for saving energy and money through the cold months, as well as energy-saving investments that can provide savings over the long term.

Energy Star

http://www.energystar.gov/

ENERGY STAR is a joint program of the U.S. Environmental Protection Agency and the U.S. Department of Energy helping us all save money and protect the environment through energy efficient products and practices.

Saving Starts @ Home: The Inside Story on Conserving Energy

http://www.ftc.gov/energysavings

This page provides a fun way to learn how you can save energy. Click on a room in the onscreen house to learn about a variety of things you can do in that room to become more energy efficient and save yourself some money. For example, in the living room the site suggests using compact fluorescent light bulbs, while in the kitchen it recommends using energy efficient appliances.

Other Money-Saving Tips

66 Ways to Save Money from the Federal Citizen Information Center

http://www.pueblo.gsa.gov/cic_text/money/66ways/index.html

This federal government site organizes savings opportunities into the following categories: transportation, insurance, banking and credit, housing, utilities, and other savings.

MyMoney.gov from the U.S. Financial Literacy and Education Commission

http://www.mymoney.gov/

MyMoney.gov is the U.S. government's website dedicated to teaching all Americans the basics about financial responsibility. Whether you are planning to buy a home, balancing your checkbook, or investing in your 401k, the resources on MyMoney.gov can help you do it better. Throughout the site, you will find important information from 20 federal agencies.

Chapter 9

What Happens When Your Check Bounces?

You bought a new stereo from the store and paid with a check. A week later you got a nasty call from the store and a fee from your bank. It turns out the check you wrote bounced. What does this mean?

✓ **Check off reasons a check might bounce.**

- ☐ Your debit card was stolen, and used by the thief before you realized it.
- ☐ You forgot to add a purchase when balancing your checkbook.
- ☐ You never balance your checkbook; you just check your balance when you do an ATM withdrawal.
- ☐ You write a check, planning to deposit another to cover it, but you don't do it in time.
- ☐ Your bank made a mistake, and your account shows less money than it should.
- ☐ Someone writes you a bad check. You don't realize it, and write your own checks from money that's not there.

Goals:

1) Learn about the penalties and legal implications of bouncing checks.
2) Learn about ChexSystems, and how bounced checks can affect your record or credit.
3) Learn how to balance your checkbook.

Use Chapters 30, 31, and 32 of Starting Out!®, the resources in this chapter, and your own Internet research to complete the following.

Bouncing a check is not fun—not only is your checking account empty, but there are other possible consequences. In some instances, you can be charged with a civil penalty, and if you intentionally write a bad check, you can be charged with a more severe, criminal penalty. In all cases, your bank will charge a fee of at least $20, and the merchant will often charge you a penalty fee as well. Using the National Check Fraud Center link in the Resources section, research your state's civil and criminal penalties for bouncing a check and describe them below.

Civil:

_____

_____

Criminal:

_____

_____

Retailers, banks, and other companies don't like to do business with someone who bounces checks regularly. How do they get this information? Bad checks are normally not on a traditional credit report, unless someone has taken legal action against you. However, a company may obtain a special consumer report from agencies such as ChexSystems or Telecheck, which collect banking information about consumers. Go to *www.consumerdebit.com/consumerinfo/us/en/chexsystems/SampleChexCnsrRpt.pdf* to view a sample report.

How long does this information stay in ChexSystems' records?

_____

_____

Can you view your own report? How much does it cost?

_____

_____

What type of information is provided in the report? List four items:

      1) _____

      2) _____

      3) _____

      4) _____

If you have negative information on your report, what is one potential consequence?

_____

_____

_____

_____

Moving forward, bouncing a check is not something you want to happen. The best way to prevent this unpleasant situation is to keep careful records of the money going into and out of your bank account by balancing your checkbook. Using Chapter 31 of Starting Out!®, the list of transactions on the next page, and a calculator, fill out this blank check register, which has an opening balance of $500:

Check Number or Debit Type	Date	Paid to	Check/Debit Amount	Deposit Amount	Balance
					$500

June 6: You wrote a check to pay your electric bill: check # 125 for $28.75 to Sunrise Electric.

June 7: You bought groceries with your debit card: $35.25.

June 8: You went out for pizza. Debit amount: $20.05

June 8: You also paid the phone and Internet bill: check #126 for $55.70 to The Phone Company.

June 9: You got gas for your car. Debit amount: $30

June 10: You got paid! Deposit amount: $500

June 10: You took out $50 from the ATM and you went out for dinner and a movie (hint: treat this as a debit).

June 11: You got the oil changed in your car: check #127 for $35 to Quick-Oil.

June 11: You took $30 out at the ATM and paid for admission to the beach and food at the snack stand.

After these purchases and deposits, what is your final balance?

_____

 **Resources**

Federal Reserve: Protecting Yourself From Overdraft and Bounced-Check Fees

http://www.federalreserve.gov/pubs/bounce/

A discussion of check overdrafts, how they occur, and what you can do to avoid them is presented at this website by the Federal Reserve. There is also a section on "courtesy" overdraft protection that some banks offer by giving you a back-up line of credit.

National Check Fraud Center: Laws and Penalties by State

http://www.ckfraud.org/penalties.html

If you think bouncing a check is not a big deal, visit this website. You can navigate to every state and learn about civil and criminal penalties for this problem, known as check fraud. Normally, if you did not intend to write a bad check, you will not have a big problem, other than paying a penalty of $25 or $30 for issuing a check backed by insufficient funds. This site addresses knowingly writing a bad check and the consequences of that action.

Chapter 10

The Pros and Cons of Credit Cards

You've started a new job and are thinking about getting a credit card. But is this really a sensible idea? Some of your friends get free airline miles and coupons for their credit card purchases, which seems like a good thing. You don't have a lot of money, though, so should you be spending money you don't actually have?

✓ Check off all that are true:

☐ Many credit cards charge more than 18 percent interest on your balance.

☐ A credit card company won't change the rate of interest if you pay on time.

☐ You have to have good credit to get a credit card.

☐ Carrying a credit card balance makes sense, as long as you always pay the minimum amount due.

☐ Credit cards should be treated like loans, which need to be paid back as soon as you can.

☐ A credit card can go toward establishing good credit to purchase items like a car or house.

Goals:

1) Learn who is eligible for a credit card.
2) Learn about interest charges and minimum payments.
3) Learn about the risks of carrying too much credit.
4) Learn about getting a secured card and other ways of building good credit.
5) Learn about your credit score — where to find it and how it affects you.
6) Compare different cards to find the best deal.
7) Identify the terms on a credit card statement.

Use Chapter 33 and 34 of Starting Out!®, the resources in this chapter, and your own Internet research to complete the following.

First, use your Starting Out!® handbook and the Internet to define some basic credit terms:

Annual Percentage Rate (APR):

_____

_____

Finance Charges:

_____

_____

Grace period:

_____

_____

Minimum payment:

_____

_____

It seems like just about anyone can sign up for a credit card, but there must be some rules. Who exactly is eligible for a credit card?

_____

Can you have too much credit? If so, why is this a problem?

_____

What is a credit score? What do you need it for? How is it calculated?

_____

_____

_____

What are some ways to build good credit?

_____

_____

What should you do if your credit card is stolen?

_____

_____

You have a credit card with a balance of $500 and an interest rate of 15 percent. How long will it take you to pay off this balance with a minimum payment of $20 a month? What if you paid $50 a month? Go to *http://www.bankrate.com/credit-cards.aspx* and enter the balance, interest rate, and payment amount under "What will it take to pay off my credit card?" How many years (divide number of months by 12) will it take to pay off your card at:

$20/month: _____ $50/ month: _____

In each case, how much will it actually cost to pay off your $500 balance? Visit *http://www.bankrate.com/credit-cards.aspx* and enter the balance, interest rate, and length of years under "The true cost of paying minimum."

Calculate the total amount paid (original debt plus interest) at:

$20/month: _____ $50/ month: _____

Is paying the minimum amount a good idea? Why or why not?

_____

_____

Where can you seek help if you get into too much credit card debt?

_____

Before choosing a credit card, you should compare a few of them side-by-side.

Go online and find the following information about three different cards. Which one, if any, would you choose? Why?

_____

Card Name	1	2	3
Introductory Rate			
Intro Period			
Regular Rate			
Credit Limit			
Application Fee			
Annual Fee			
Late Fee			
Result of Going Over Limit			
Online Bill Payment-yes or no			
Grace Period Before Interest Charged			
Other Features			

 **Resources**

Federal Reserve Board: Choosing a Credit Card
http://www.federalreserve.gov/Pubs/shop/

Seven useful selections cover aspects of credit cards, including usage, fees and finance charges, credit limits, grace periods, damaged goods, and complaints.

Federal Trade Commission: Choosing a Credit Card: The Deal Is in the Disclosures
http://www.ftc.gov/bcp/edu/pubs/consumer/credit/cre05.shtm

The FTC offers this useful glossary of credit card terms and Balance Computation Methods for those seeking a full understanding of credit card procedures.

College Board: Credit Card Smarts
http://www.collegeboard.com/student/plan/college-success/9139.html

A discussion of credit cards relative to student use is provided by the College Board, including an explanation of terminology, information about credit reports, and "credit-smart" recommendations, such as using a debit card whenever possible.

Chapter 11

Combating Identity Theft, Scams, and Fraud

Y̶ou're reviewing your credit card bill when you notice that a TV has been charged to it. You didn't purchase the TV—someone must have stolen your information! How did this happen? What should you do?

Goals:

1) Learn what to do about erroneous charges.
2) Learn about identity theft and what you should do if you suspect that your identity's been stolen.
3) Learn about fraud and scams.
4) Learn what you can do to protect yourself.

Use Chapter 35 of Starting Out!®, the resources in this chapter, and your own Internet research to complete the following.

If you discover erroneous charges on your bill or statement, your identity may have been stolen. In the event that your credit card, debit card, or other identity information is being used by someone else, you need to take certain steps to rectify the situation. Please number the following items so that they're in the correct order, starting with step one and ending with step five.

Number 1 through 5

☐ Write a follow-up statement to the company, indicating that you did not charge the item in question.

☐ Call the three national credit-reporting agencies to report the theft of your credit information.

☐ Report the identity theft to the local police.

☐ Call the company issuing the card to report the theft and ask for a freeze on the account.

☐ Contact the Social Security Administration if you suspect that your Social Security number has been taken.

How quickly should you contact your credit card company or bank?

_____

Fortunately, there are federal laws that help protect consumers from credit or debit card theft. Under the Fair Credit Billing Act, what is the maximum amount you could owe after a card theft?

_____

More and more, identity theft is becoming a concern. With identity theft, not only are bank and credit card information stolen, but thieves may also assume your name and social security number and commit crimes with them. What are two ways in which your identity might be stolen?

1) _____

2) _____

What are two things thieves could do with your identity? There are many court cases with examples.

1) _____

2) _____

Beyond identity theft, frauds and scams are other issues to be concerned about. Using the resources listed at the end of this chapter, write down three frauds or scams that you should be alert for:

1) _____

2) _____

3) _____

Another thing to watch out for is a specific type of scam called phishing. What is phishing?

_____
_____
_____

Fortunately, there are many things you can do to protect yourself from fraud, scams, and identity theft. Just using common sense will go a long way. What are some other tips you could offer a friend or family member to help them protect their identity and avoid scams?

Identity Theft Tip #1:	
Identity Theft Tip #2:	
Fraud/Scam Tip #1:	
Fraud/Scam Tip #2:	

 **Resources**

Identity Theft

FTC: Credit, ATM, and Debit Cards: What to do if They're Lost or Stolen

http://www.ftc.gov/bcp/edu/pubs/consumer/credit/cre04.shtm

Sound advice from the Federal Trade Commission related to lost or stolen credit cards, pin numbers, and debit cards is offered on this website. There is a discussion of limited financial exposure, along with guidelines to help prevent others from gaining access to your personal credit information.

The Federal Trade Commission's Identity Theft Site

http://www.ftc.gov/bcp/edu/microsites/idtheft

To fight identity theft, a huge growing problem worldwide, the U.S. Federal Trade Commission offers this website to help you learn about this crime and defend yourself. Terms such as "phishing" are explained, and advice is given about actions to take if you suspect that your identity has been compromised or stolen.

Scams and Fraud

National Consumer League: Fraud Center

http://www.fraud.org/

Resources for consumers on Internet fraud, telemarketing fraud, business scams, scams against the elderly, and counterfeit drugs can be found at this non-profit organization's website.

Federal Citizen Information Center: Scams and Frauds

http://www.pueblo.gsa.gov/scamsdesc.htm

Different types of scams and frauds are explained at this government website, including those dealing with cars, computers, education, employment, and other areas.

National Credit-Reporting Agencies

Three national credit reporting services maintain detailed records on individual credit in the U.S., and establish ratings for everyone listed. If you have been the subject of a scam, fraud, or identity theft, you can report this information to these three agencies so they note the incident in your records.

Equifax: 1–800–525–6285
Experian (formerly TRW): 1–888–397–3742
Trans Union: 1–800–680–7289

Chapter 12

Learning About Saving and Investing

Y ou have some extra money saved up, and you want to learn how to invest some of it. You've heard that investing your money can help it grow, but what should you do with it? You could put some in the stock market or get a certificate of deposit (CD). What are some other options for saving and investing your money? Check any investment approaches you are using now:

✓ **Check All That Apply**

- ☐ Savings account
- ☐ Interest checking
- ☐ Bonds
- ☐ Mutual funds
- ☐ Bank CD
- ☐ Insured money market accounts
- ☐ Stocks

Goals:

1) Learn about saving and investing.
2) Learn about risk vs. return.
3) Explore asset allocation, compounding interest, and other financial principles.
4) Learn about mutual funds and other classes of investment.
5) Learn how to read the U.S. stock market pages.

Use Part VIII of Starting Out!®, the resources in this chapter, and your own Internet research to complete the following.

Some people you know don't even have a savings account. Why should you consider saving or investing money, anyway?

_____

_____

_____

_____

Some investment products—such as bank accounts, CDs, and insured money market accounts—have a low risk and return. What does this mean?

_____

_____

_____

Even with a low risk and return, compounded interest can add up over time. Use the savings calculator at _http://apps.finra.org/investor_Information/Calculators/1/SavingsCalc.aspx_ to compare saving $20 a month for one year with no interest, with an annual percentage yield of 2 percent, and with an annual percentage yield of 4 percent. Start with $500 and assume no inflation. How much money is in the account after one year?

No interest: _____

2% interest: _____

4% interest: _____

Conversely, other products have a higher risk and return. Define the following examples of higher risk and return products:

Mutual funds:_____

Bonds: _____

Stocks: _____

What are two ways to earn money with stocks?

1) _____

2) _____

Asset allocation and diversification are two ways to lower the risk of investing. What are the definitions of asset allocation and diversification?

Asset allocation: _____

Diversification: _____

If you decide to buy some stocks, you will need to know how to follow their value. Go to one of the sites in the resources section, and look up the current values of three stocks. Then fill out the chart below:

Company Name	Company Symbol	Current Price	Price Range Over One Year	Today's Gain / Loss in Points	Today's Percentage Gain / Loss

 **Resources**

The SEC's Roadmap to Saving and Investing
http://www.sec.gov/investor/pubs/roadmap.htm

Saving and investing require care and skill. Learn about defining your goals and making a financial plan. Then, determine your risk tolerance for different types of saving and investment products. Get financial advice from professionals.

MyMoney.gov: Saving and Investing
http://www.mymoney.gov

Read useful articles about investing, finding and checking out brokers, costs of investing, credit unions, and much more. This website has information for different ages and stages of life, calculators, and financial planning principles.

Chapter 13

April 15th is Approaching. That Means Tax Time!

April 15th is getting closer and closer, and your friends at work are talking about preparing their tax returns. You know that you need to pay taxes, but you don't know where to start. And what are all those forms you got in the mail?

Goals:

1) Learn about different tax forms.
2) Learn about federal taxes.
3) Learn about state taxes.
4) Learn how to prepare and file taxes.

Use Part IX of Starting Out!®, the resources in this chapter, and your own Internet research to complete the following.

Anyone who earns above a minimum amount of money over the course of the year will need to pay taxes on that money. Taxes, as defined by the Internal Revenue Service, are: _____
_____

What types of income are taxable?

- [ ] Wages earned working in an office
- [ ] Tips received by a food server
- [ ] Wages earned by working part-time at a local gym
- [ ] $100 gift certificate from Grandma
- [ ] Interest from a savings account

When you start a job, you will have to fill out a Form W-4, Employee's Withholding Allowance Certificate. This form allows your employer to determine how much income tax should be withheld from your paycheck. Typically, a single person specifies one allowance.

By the end of January, your employer(s) will give you a Form W-2, Wage and Tax Statement, like the one shown below, which explains all the money that has been deducted from your annual earnings.

a Employee's social security number 123-45-6789	OMB No. 1545-0008	Safe, accurate, FAST! Use	Visit the IRS website at www.irs.gov/efile.

b Employer identification number (EIN) 987-65-4321		1 Wages, tips, other compensation 16,700.00	2 Federal income tax withheld 985.00
c Employer's name, address, and ZIP code Your local bookstore 5 River Road Anytown, US xxxxx		3 Social security wages 16,700.00	4 Social security tax withheld 1,036.14
		5 Medicare wages and tips 16,700.00	6 Medicare tax withheld 242.19
		7 Social security tips	8 Allocated tips
d Control number		9 Advance EIC payment	10 Dependent care benefits
e Employee's first name and initial Last name Suff. Robin N. Bateman 100 Main Street Anytown, US xxxxx	11 Nonqualified plans		12a See instructions for box 12
	13 Statutory employee ☐ Retirement plan ☐ Third-party sick pay ☐		12b
	14 Other		12c
			12d
f Employee's address and ZIP code			

15 State US	Employer's state ID number 987-65-4321	16 State wages, tips, etc. 16,700.00	17 State income tax 400.44	18 Local wages, tips, etc.	19 Local income tax	20 Locality name

Form **W-2** Wage and Tax Statement   **2008**   Department of the Treasury—Internal Revenue Service

Copy B—To Be Filed With Employee's FEDERAL Tax Return.
This information is being furnished to the Internal Revenue Service.

To figure out if you owe taxes or if you are entitled to a refund, you will fill out a federal and a state tax form. Your taxable income is equal to your total income minus any deductions. Your tax due can then be computed, using tables at IRS.gov. Subtract your withholding amount from your tax owed, and you will find out if you owe money or are getting a refund.

You can choose a standard deduction, or itemize your deductions if their total is greater than the standard. Deductions include items such as donations to charity, interest on student loans or home mortgages, real estate taxes, and certain job-related expenses.

You can use several different tax forms to pay your federal income tax. The most basic federal tax form is Form 1040EZ Income Tax Return, which only lets you use the standard deduction. If you would like to claim more deductions, you need to use a longer form. For this example, use the above information to fill out this sample Form 1040EZ. You will find a tax table at *http://www.irs.gov/pub/irs-pdf/i1040ez.pdf.*

Form
1040EZ

Department of the Treasury—Internal Revenue Service

Income Tax Return for Single and Joint Filers With No Dependents (99) **2008**

OMB No. 1545-0074

Label

(See page 9.)

Use the IRS label.

Otherwise, please print or type.

Presidential Election Campaign (page 9)

L A B E L   H E R E

Your first name and initial	Last name	Your social security number
If a joint return, spouse's first name and initial	Last name	Spouse's social security number
Home address (number and street). If you have a P.O. box, see page 9.	Apt. no.	▲ You **must** enter your SSN(s) above. ▲
City, town or post office, state, and ZIP code. If you have a foreign address, see page 9.		Checking a box below will not change your tax or refund.

Check here if you, or your spouse if a joint return, want $3 to go to this fund . . . ▶ ☐ **You**   ☐ **Spouse**

Income

Attach Form(s) W-2 here.

Enclose, but do not attach, any payment.

1 Wages, salaries, and tips. This should be shown in box 1 of your Form(s) W-2. Attach your Form(s) W-2. | 1 |

2 Taxable interest. If the total is over $1,500, you cannot use Form 1040EZ. | 2 |

3 Unemployment compensation and Alaska Permanent Fund dividends (see page 11). | 3 |

4 Add lines 1, 2, and 3. This is your **adjusted gross income.** | 4 |

5 If someone can claim you (or your spouse if a joint return) as a dependent, check the applicable box(es) below and enter the amount from the worksheet on back.

☐ **You**   ☐ **Spouse**

If no one can claim you (or your spouse if a joint return), enter $8,950 if **single;** $17,900 if **married filing jointly.** See back for explanation. | 5 |

6 Subtract line 5 from line 4. If line 5 is larger than line 4, enter -0-. This is your **taxable income.** ▶ | 6 |

Payments and tax

7 Federal income tax withheld from box 2 of your Form(s) W-2. | 7 |

8a **Earned income credit (EIC)** (see page 12). | 8a |

b Nontaxable combat pay election. | 8b |

9 Recovery rebate credit (see worksheet on pages 17 and 18). | 9 |

10 Add lines 7, 8a, and 9. These are your **total payments.** ▶ | 10 |

11 **Tax.** Use the amount on **line 6 above** to find your tax in the tax table on pages 28–36 of the booklet. Then, enter the tax from the table on this line. | 11 |

Refund

Have it directly deposited! See page 18 and fill in 12b, 12c, and 12d or Form 8888.

12a If line 10 is larger than line 11, subtract line 11 from line 10. This is your **refund.** If Form 8888 is attached, check here ▶ ☐ | 12a |

▶ b Routing number ▶ c Type: ☐ Checking ☐ Savings

▶ d Account number

Amount you owe

13 If line 11 is larger than line 10, subtract line 10 from line 11. This is the **amount you owe.** For details on how to pay, see page 19. ▶ | 13 |

Third party designee

Do you want to allow another person to discuss this return with the IRS (see page 20)? ☐ **Yes.** Complete the following. ☐ **No**

| Designee's name ▶ | Phone no. ▶ ( ) | Personal identification number (PIN) ▶ |

Sign here

Joint return? See page 6.

Keep a copy for your records.

Under penalties of perjury, I declare that I have examined this return, and to the best of my knowledge and belief, it is true, correct, and accurately lists all amounts and sources of income I received during the tax year. Declaration of preparer (other than the taxpayer) is based on all information of which the preparer has any knowledge.

| Your signature | Date | Your occupation | Daytime phone number ( ) |
| Spouse's signature. If a joint return, **both** must sign. | Date | Spouse's occupation | |

Paid preparer's use only

Preparer's signature ▶	Date	Check if self-employed ☐	Preparer's SSN or PTIN
Firm's name (or yours if self-employed), address, and ZIP code ▶		EIN	
		Phone no. ( )	

For Disclosure, Privacy Act, and Paperwork Reduction Act Notice, see page 37.   Cat. No. 11329W   Form **1040EZ** (2008)

Does Robin owe taxes, or will she receive a refund? How much?

Most states also have a state income tax. State taxes work much like federal taxes, though specific forms will vary from state to state. Print out a copy of your state tax form, and use the W-2 to calculate Robin's state taxes.

Gross adjusted income (from Form 1040EZ):	
Taxable income (minus deductions and exemptions):	
State taxes owed (find this through your state revenue service):	
State taxes withheld:	
Taxes due, or refund? How much?	

 **Resources**

The IRS Website: All About Taxes
http://www.irs.gov/individuals/index.html

Through this Internal Revenue Service website, you can get answers to numerous questions, learn about tax obligations and filing procedures, and begin to understand how taxes work.

Internal Revenue Service: Tax Information for Students
http://www.irs.gov/individuals/students/index.html

Students can learn about taxes and when they need to file their own tax return. This section of the IRS website offers extensive information so students can learn the rules and start off on the right track.

GovSpot.com: State Departments of Revenue
http://www.govspot.com/tax/staterevenue.htm

This website has a convenient list of links to each state revenue department. Learn about the tax rates and filing obligations in any state.

Chapter 14

Renting a Place and Signing a Lease

Now that you have a job, you'd like to have a place of your own. You know where you want to live, but how do you find out what housing is available? Should you get a roommate? What's a security deposit? What are the "dos" and "don'ts" of renting?

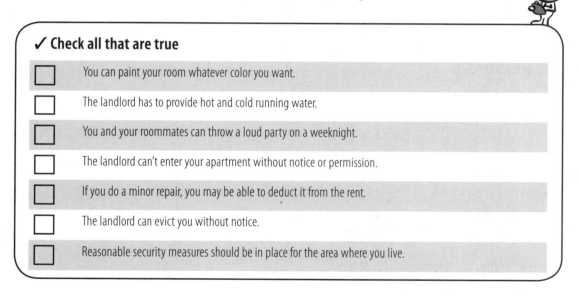

✓ Check all that are true

- [ ] You can paint your room whatever color you want.
- [ ] The landlord has to provide hot and cold running water.
- [ ] You and your roommates can throw a loud party on a weeknight.
- [ ] The landlord can't enter your apartment without notice or permission.
- [ ] If you do a minor repair, you may be able to deduct it from the rent.
- [ ] The landlord can evict you without notice.
- [ ] Reasonable security measures should be in place for the area where you live.

Goals:

1) Learn how to find out about available rental properties.
2) Learn about signing a lease and what to look for before signing.
3) Learn about security deposits and how to get yours back.
4) Learn about renters' insurance and liability issues.
5) Learn about what utilities you need, which ones you want, and how to get them.
6) Learn about the advantages and disadvantages of having a roommate.

Use Chapters 42 and 43 of Starting Out!®, the resources in this chapter, and your own Internet research to complete the following.

The first step in getting your own place is to locate available rentals. Use one of the websites listed in the Resources section, or another that you've found independently, to carry out a search for an apartment in your area. Enter the apartment address below:

_____

If you have some friends who are also looking for a place to live, you may want to consider asking them to be roommates. What are the pros and cons of having roommates?

Pros:

1) _____

2) _____

Cons:

1) _____

2) _____

To rent an apartment, you will need to sign a lease, which will contain all of the terms of the rental agreement. Leases need to be read carefully, so that you understand all the fine print. For example, if you have a dog, you would want to make sure that pets are allowed. Look at the sample lease provided on the last page of this chapter and answer the following questions:

When does the lease begin?	
What is the address of the property?	
How much is the monthly rent?	
How much is the security deposit?	
Is the apartment furnished?	
How many cars may be parked in the lot?	
By what time do you need to finish your piano practice?	
How can you decorate your walls?	
Can you bring your dog?	
How can the lease be terminated?	

Before you move in, the landlord will ask for a security deposit. In theory, this money will be returned to you when your lease ends, provided that you don't owe any rent and no damage beyond reasonable wear and tear has been done to the unit. Otherwise, the money will be used to alleviate those problems. What are some things you can do to make sure your security deposit is returned?

1) _____

2) _____

3) _____

The property you bring with you to your new place has value, and could be difficult to replace if your belongings get damaged or stolen. Should you consider renters insurance? Why or why not?

_____

_____

_____

Finally, before you move in, you need to contact the local utility companies and ask for them to turn their services on, and/or put the billing information in your name. Some utilities can be considered essentials—most people can't get by without heat, water, sewer, telephone service, and electricity. Other utilities, such as cable TV and Internet service, could be considered non-essential. Using the web, locate the contact information of your local essential utility companies:

Electric company:	
Water provider:	
Sewer provider:	
Telephone service (land line or cell):	
Heat provider (this could be oil, gas, wood, or electricity. Choose the one that is common for your area):	

Resources

Apartments.com
http://www.apartments.com

You can search nationwide by state for apartments at this website, then by region, county, and city or town to find specific offerings in any area of the country.

Rent.com
http://www.rent.com/rentals/

Rent.com, like Apartments.com, offers a search engine to locate apartments in every region of the country. After selecting a state, you narrow down the search by specifying a region and city or town using maps until you are looking at actual listings in the desired area. There are photos of apartments, rental rates, and descriptions of housing complexes.

Sublet.com
http://www.sublet.com

For people seeking to sub-let an apartment anywhere in the United States and around the world, Sublet.com offers a search engine and free tenant access. The user can drill down from region or state to area to city or town to locate prospective available apartments to rent. Sublets can often be cheaper than signing a direct lease because the original renter may have moved but remains responsible under the lease until the term ends.

Tenant Rights from the Department of Housing & Urban Development (HUD)
http://www.hud.gov/renting/tenantrights.cfm

A directory at this HUD website offers links to tenant rights information for every state, including landlord-tenant laws, smoking regulations, legal assistance, and state housing advisory agencies.

Apartment Lease Guide from the University of Pittsburgh
http://www.ocl.pitt.edu/rental/lease-guide.html

This guide to off-campus housing offered by the University of Pittsburgh offers useful information to learn about the rental process, including lease information, security deposits, rules and regulations, rights of use and occupancy, landlord entry rights, and other information for those seeking an apartment.

Insurance Information Institute: Homeowners and Renters Insurance
http://www.iii.org/individuals/HomeownersandRentersInsurance/

The Insurance Information Institute is a non-profit industry association that offers information on all types of insurance. On this page there is a discussion of homeowners and renters insurance, for people seeking to protect their personal property from theft, fire, and other types of damage.

Sample Apartment Lease Agreement

Issue Date: June 8, 2010
Lease Commencement Date: June 15, 2010
Lease Termination Date: June 14, 2011

Landlord Name: Bill Smith
Lessee Name: Bob Jones

This Lease Agreement is for the property and term described below in consideration of payment of a $300.00 deposit which must be received by the Landlord on or before the date this contract is signed.

Address: 15 Main Street, Apt B, Portland, ME 04101
Furnishings: Unfurnished
Rent: Lessee agrees to pay $600.00 per month for rental. Rent is due in advance on the first day of each month.
Utilities: The following utilities are provided by UTA and are included in the rent: Gas/Water/UTA Ethernet/Basic Cable TV/UTA Phone. Lessee shall pay for all other utilities and related deposits except as noted above.

Additional Occupant Name: Tim Wilson
Move in Date: June 15th 2010

Special Considerations:

In Assignment and Subletting: The Lessee shall not assign this Lease or sublet the Premises without the prior written consent of the Landlord, which consent shall not be arbitrarily or unreasonably withheld. The Landlord shall be entitled to reimbursement by the Lessee for any reasonable expenses incurred in connection with the granting of any such consent.
Parking: The Lessee shall have the right to park two automobiles in the parking lot outside the Building.
Noise: Noise of any kind which in the opinion of the landlord may be calculated to disturb the comfort of any other occupant of the building shall not be made by the Lessee, nor shall any noise whatsoever including the playing of any musical instrument be repeated or persisted in after requests to discontinue such noise has been given by the landlord. Pianos, organs, violins, and other musical instruments shall not be permitted to be played by the Lessee in the premises after eleven o'clock p.m.
Walls: The Lessee shall not paint, paper or decorate any part of the premises without first obtaining the consent of the Landlord. Spikes, hooks, nails or screws shall not be inserted in the walls or floors or woodwork of the premises.
Animals: Pets are not allowed, with the exception of fish in an aquarium of 15 gallons or less in size.

Overdue Rent and Returned Checks: The Lessee agrees to pay to the Landlord interest on overdue Rent payments at the rate of 15% per annum, compounded monthly. The Lessee also agrees to pay to the Landlord a service charge of $30.00 for each check tendered to the Landlord which is not honored.

Rent Increases and Lease Changes: No rent increases or other lease changes shall be allowed during the above stated lease term. For rent increases or other lease changes effective at the end of the lease term or renewal period, at least 30 days notice to lessee is required.

Notice of Termination of Tenancy: If either the Landlord or the Lessee desire to terminate the tenancy at the expiration or end of the Term, he shall give notice in writing to that effect to the other party 30 days prior to the expiration of such Term or in accordance with the provisions of any applicable laws.

Landlord Signature and Date:
Lessee Signature and Date:

Chapter 15

Buying vs. Renting: All About Housing Options

Now that you have a steady job, you are considering buying your first house or condominium. You love the idea of having a place that you actually own, a place where you can make the changes you want. You're even excited about mowing the lawn. But is buying a house a better option than renting? How do you start the process? Do you need a real estate agent?

Goals:

1) Learn about the pros and cons of buying and renting.
2) Learn about finding houses and properties.
3) Learn about what to look for in a house, particularly during the inspection.
4) Learn about mortgages and government home buying programs.
5) Learn about closing costs.

Use Chapters 44 and 45 from Starting Out!®, the resources in this chapter, and your own Internet research to complete the following.

First, you need to decide if buying a home is right for you. Fill in the following chart to compare the advantages and disadvantages of buying versus renting a home.

	Advantages	Disadvantages/Risks
Buying a Home		
Renting a Home		

If you've decided that the time is right to buy a home, you will need to choose that home. You can do this independently, or you can find a real estate broker. Which would you choose, and why?

_____

_____

_____

Even if you sign on with a realtor, you can still look for houses on your own. Do an online search for real estate finders in your state and write the names of two real estate websites below.

1) _____

2) _____

When buying a home, you need to determine the town, city, or neighborhood where you'd like to live and the features that are essential to you. Consider some of these factors.

In what other area in your state (other than your current address) would you like to live?

_____

_____

Would you prefer a house, a condominium, or some other type of home? Would you prefer a newer or older home?

_____

_____

_____

List six essential features you would like your home to have:

1:	
2:	
3:	
4:	
5:	
6:	

One important thing to do before you start seriously searching is to think about a mortgage, or loan for a property. Prequalification with a reputable lender, such as a trustworthy bank, will let you know how much you can borrow and at what rate of interest. Find a bank in your area and its current mortgage rates.

Bank name: _____

Rate for a 30-year fixed-rate mortgage: _____

What is the difference between a fixed-rate mortgage and an adjustable-rate mortgage (ARM)?

_____

_____

_____

The government also offers a number of loan or assistance programs to help you fulfill your dream of home ownership. Find a home-buyer program available in your state that you might qualify for and describe it below.

_____

_____

_____

_____

You've been prequalified for a loan, researched homeownership programs, found the home you'd like, and have taken the next step, making an offer. At this point you need to carry out an important part of the homebuying process: getting an inspection. This process involves an evaluation of the home's condition by a qualified inspector. What are two good reasons to get a home inspection?

1) _____

2) _____

When you receive a contract, have an attorney review it. After you've signed a contract and secured your mortgage, your lender will set up a closing date, when the property will officially change hands. Aside from getting a deed and signing papers for the mortgage, you should be prepared for certain extra closing costs. List three of these charges below:

1) _____

2) _____

3) _____

 **Resources**

Should You Rent or Own?

http://militaryfinance.umuc.edu/debt/debtworks_rent.html

A handy comparison of the pros and cons of renting and buying are presented at this University of Maryland website. Numerous issues must be considered in making a decision between these two options, including your financial situation, your time horizon at this location, market prices, the ability to resell if needed, risks of homeownership, and much more.

GinnieMae.org: Buying vs. Renting
http://www.ginniemae.gov/

Scroll down the opening page of this site and visit the Homeownership Section. Use the calculators to compare the advantages and considerations of buying vs. renting a home. Can you afford to buy? What are the risks? Do you have the down payment needed?

HUD: 100 Questions & Answers About Buying a Home
http://www.hud.gov/offices/hsg/sfh/buying/buyhm.cfm

From looking for possible homes to buy to mortgage financing questions and then to closing, this website offers an orderly and clear explanation of the steps involved in buying a home, in a convenient question and answer format.

American Society of Home Inspectors: Frequently Asked Questions on Home Inspections
http://www.ashi.org/customers/faq.asp

Home inspections are of critical importance in purchasing a property. Be sure you use a certified home inspector, and try to accompany the inspector during his or her entire examination of the property to learn about problems that may exist.

American Bar Association: Buying or Selling a Home: The Closing
http://www.abanet.org/publiced/practical/homeclosing_costs.html

The American Bar Association has provided a useful summary of common closing costs that must be paid at a home purchase closing. All of these items together may cost several thousand dollars. Also, click on "There can't possibly be any more closing fees, can there?" for more information.

Chapter 16

The Ins and Outs of Buying a Vehicle

You're tired of driving around in the same old car you've had since high school. You know you want a car that's reliable and safe, but you also want a car that has a look that appeals to you. How do you find out about different cars, including mileage performance? Should you buy a new or a used car? What does it mean to lease a car?

Goals:

1) Compare the pros and cons of buying a new or a used car.
2) Compare buying vs. leasing a vehicle.
3) Learn about different car brands, models, and features, such as EPA gas ratings.
4) Learn about financing a car.
5) Learn about insurance, including how much you need.
6) Learn about registering your car.

Use Chapter 26 of Starting Out!®, the resources in this chapter, and your own Internet research to complete the following.

The first thing you need to decide is whether you'd like to get a new or used car. Fill in the following chart to compare the pros and cons of new and used cars. Think about issues such as price, safety, and dependability.

	New Car	Used Car
Pros		
Cons		

If you choose a new car, you need to decide whether you prefer to lease it or buy it. When you lease a car, you pay monthly for a specified term, such as two, three, or four years. You can think of it as a very long term rental. List two advantages and two disadvantages of leasing a car, rather than buying one.

Leasing a Car	
Advantage I	
Advantage II	
Disadvantage I	
Disadvantage II	

When you buy a car, you need to decide what features are important to you. Check off all that apply:

✓ Features that are important to me:

☐	Fuel economy
☐	Transmission type (manual vs. automatic)
☐	Engine size
☐	4-wheel drive
☐	Air conditioning
☐	Power windows and doors
☐	Safety: front and side airbags, side impact bars, automated braking system, etc.
☐	Comfort
☐	Warranty

Now choose your top three features. Using a websites listed in the Resources section, compare two cars of your choosing in the table below.

Feature	Car #1:	Car #2:

Which car better suits your preferences?

Now that you have chosen a car, you need to pay for it. While some people have the option of paying cash for their vehicle, most often the purchase is financed by taking out a loan. While used cars cost less, used car loans often have a higher interest rate and must be paid off over a shorter term than new car loans. So, it is often worthwhile to compare used and new car purchases. The table below will take you through the process of making this comparison.

Use *www.maineautomall.com/section_Find_A_Car_4*, or a car dealership website from your state, to find out prices and monthly payments. You can also call a local dealership. Find interest rates for your state at *www.bankrate. com/auto.aspx* or call a local bank; be sure to choose the best rate from a local bank. Assume a $1,000 down payment.

Make and Model (from above):						
	Length of Loan	Price	Financing (Interest Rate)	Down Payment	Monthly Payments	Total Paid Over Life of Loan (payment x months)
New Car						
Year: 2010						
	48 Months			$1,000		
	72 Months			$1,000		
Used Car						
Year: 2005						
	24 Months*			$1,000		
	36 Months*			$1,000		

Used car loans are usually shorter than new car loans, since you are likely to replace the car more quickly.

Which car and loan option do you feel is the best for you? Why?

_____

Now that you have chosen and determined how you will pay for your car, you need to insure and register it. What is liability coverage, and what is the recommended amount of liability coverage in your state?

_____

_____

_____

Something else to consider when insuring your car is whether or not you would like to insure the value of your car against accident damage. If you were in an accident, would you want to be reimbursed for your repair costs?

_____

_____

_____

In your state, where do you register your car?

_____

_____

What do you need to bring with you, if this is the first time you're registering this vehicle?

_____

_____

_____

 **Resources**

Buying and Selling
Kelley Blue Book
http://www.kbb.com/

The Kelley Blue Book is a guide to new and used car values. This website allows the visitor to enter information on any make or model car and find its current value.

NADA Guides: Compare Cars
http://www.nadaguides.com

This is a comprehensive vehicle information website, with extensive information on cars and models. Use it to research vehicles and evaluate possible purchases.

DMV.org: Buying and Selling
http://www.dmv.org/buy-sell

Useful guides to buying and selling vehicles can be found at this website. Informative articles can help you explore whether to buy or sell, and then explain the precise process.

Fuel Economy

FuelEconomy.gov: Find a Car

http://www.fueleconomy.gov/feg/findacar.htm

Do you want to know how fuel-efficient your car is? Enter your car and model and find out the expected fuel efficiency level, or research a new or used car based upon fuel economy.

Vehicle Financing

Federal Trade Commission: Financing, Leasing, or Renting

http://www.ftc.gov/bcp/menus/consumer/autos/finance.shtm

Obtain unbiased information and advice from the Federal Trade Commission before you finance a vehicle. Learn about automobile loans, as well as leasing and short-term rentals.

Leasing a Vehicle

Automotive.com: Car Leasing FAQs

http://www.automotive.com/auto-loans/36/loan-tips/car-leasing-faqs.html

Compare car leasing vs. buying on this site, and obtain reliable answers to numerous questions about leasing a car.

Registration and Titling

DMV.org: Registration and Titling

http://www.dmv.org/vehicle-registration.php

Do you want to learn how and where to register your vehicle in any state, as well as how to obtain the title? DMV.org offers helpful articles on these and numerous other subjects related to vehicle ownership.

Insurance

Insurance Information Institute: Auto Insurance

http://www.iii.org/individuals/autoinsurance/

A full explanation of auto insurance is presented by this non-profit insurance association, including clear explanations about automobile insurance companies, types of coverage, costs, liability, teen drivers, filing claims, and other important issues.

Chapter 17

Gaining Weight, Junk Food, and Nutrition

You notice that since you've been working, you've started gaining weight. Since you got your job, you occasionally eat at your parents' house, but more often than not, you're pressed for time so you grab a burger and fries for lunch, eat a chocolate bar for a snack, and have a pizza delivered for dinner. And there just doesn't seem to be time for exercise. Could these factors have something to do with it?

Which of the following may be considered junk food?

✓ Check All That Apply

☐ French fries

☐ Unsalted, unbuttered popcorn

☐ Potato chips

☐ Milk

☐ Dried apples

☐ Energy drinks

☐ Fruit roll-ups

☐ Low-fat pretzels

☐ Chocolate chip muffin

Goals:

1) Learn what is considered junk food and why junk food is unhealthy.
2) Learn about nutrition and how to eat healthy.
3) Learn about the health risks of an unhealthy diet.

Use Part XI of Starting Out!®, the resources in this chapter, and your own Internet research to complete the following.

Define the term "junk food." What are junk foods high in? What are they low in?

_____

_____

_____

List three problems with junk food:

1) _____

2) _____

3) _____

It may seem like junk food is everywhere, but it's not hard to eat a healthy diet. In fact, scientists have come up with food pyramids to help you put in perspective the quantities of each food you should eat daily. There are a number of different types of pyramids, but they all give the same basic message: eat small amounts of unhealthy foods and large amounts of healthy foods.

Create a pyramid of the types and quantities of foods you normally eat. Draw lines from the point to the base in different widths to show the quantities you eat. Create a thin triangle to show the foods you eat least; use wider triangles to list the foods you most often eat.

Here are some ideas for basic categories: Proteins, Grains, Dairy and Eggs, Fruits and Vegetables, Fats and Sugars. You can break down categories into more specific segments if you like.

Now, fill out this pyramid with the actual United States Department of Agriculture recommendations (found at www.mypyramid.gov)

Food pyramids are a good place to start to help you think about nutrition. But healthy eating goes beyond food groups. Now it's time to think about protein, carbohydrates, fats, fiber, and vitamins and minerals.

From a nutritional standpoint, why are proteins important?

_____

_____

What are the pros and cons of carbohydrates?

_____

_____

What are the pros and cons of fats?

_____

_____

What is fiber? Why do you need it?

_____

_____

How can the nutrition information on food labels help you?

_____

_____

Even with the help of nutrition labels, sometimes it seems hard to maintain a healthy diet. However, there are dangers to eating lots of junk food, or lots of food in general. List three health conditions that can be caused by an unhealthy diet.

1) _____

2) _____

3) _____

 **Resources**

My Pyramid Tracker.gov
http://www.mypyramidtracker.gov/
The Center for Nutrition Policy and Promotion provides an extensive website about the food pyramid. The site describes itself as "an online dietary and physical activity assessment tool that provides information on your diet quality, physical activity status, related nutrition issues, and links to nutritional and physical activity information.

Chapter 18

Learning to Cook and Becoming a Smart Shopper

You've been making an effort to eat at home, but all you know how to do is boil water and use the microwave. Frozen dinners and take-out food are getting old—you're ready to try something new. You never learned to cook, though, and don't know where to start. And sometimes when you do try a recipe, you don't have most of the ingredients. It seems like some of your friends are natural cooks; how did they learn?

The following are potential places to learn to cook. Check off three approaches you might consider:

✓ Check all that apply

- ☐ An adult education class
- ☐ Cooking shows on TV
- ☐ Cooking magazines
- ☐ Friends or family members
- ☐ Cookbooks
- ☐ Online classes
- ☐ Cooking websites
- ☐ Culinary school

Goals:

1) Find out how and where to learn to cook.
2) Learn about menu planning.
3) Learn about buying food and unit prices.
4) Learn about locating fresh, local food.

Use Chapter 49 of Starting Out!®, the resources in this chapter, and your own Internet research to respond to the following.

As you can see, there are many places and many ways to learn how to cook.

Two common and inexpensive ways to learn to cook are through books or websites. Do a search and locate a cookbook that sounds appealing to you. Write the title below.

_____

Now, find a cooking website (look in your Starting Out!® handbook for ideas) and look up a recipe that you'd like to learn to make.

Website: _____

Recipe: _____

Does this website teach you about cooking techniques, such as boiling pasta or steaming vegetables? If so, explore it a bit and find a cooking technique you'd like to learn. If not, try another website. Write down this cooking technique below.

_____
_____
_____
_____

Meal or menu planning means planning your meals (for a day, a week, etc.) ahead of time. How can menu planning save you time and money?

_____
_____
_____

How can menu planning make your meals healthier?

_____
_____
_____

How can menu planning make your meals more interesting?

_____
_____
_____

Do some research and plan a day's worth of meals: breakfast, lunch, and dinner. Write down what dishes you are planning to make, and then make a list of your ingredients. This would be your shopping list.

Breakfast:	
Lunch:	
Dinner:	
Shopping List:	

While shopping, there are a number of different factors to keep in mind when selecting an item, especially since there are so many brands to choose from. What are two things to consider when purchasing a food item?

1) _____

2) _____

When evaluating the cost of similar items, it is important to look beyond the overall price and compare products by unit price. The unit price tells you how much something costs based on its weight or volume—this lets you better compare the cost and value of your selections.

For example, if you buy an 8-oz. bag of pretzels for $2.80, it will cost you $.35/ounce. A 12-oz. bag for $3.60 might cost more, but the unit price is $.30/ounce, giving you more pretzels for your money.

Now it's your turn. In the example below which is the best deal for a container of orange juice? Figure out the answer by calculating the unit price per quart. **Circle your answer.**

$1.00 for one quart

$1.80 for one half gallon

$2.80 for one gallon

While many foods can only be grown in certain parts of the country or world, each region has many items that can be grown and harvested locally. What are the nutritional benefits of buying local food?

_____
_____
_____
_____

What are the economic benefits of buying local food?

_____

_____

_____

Look online and write down the name of one place in your area where you can buy local food, such as a local farm, farmers' market, or supermarket.

_____

 **Resources**

Cooking and Meal Planning
Shopping, Cooking & Meal Planning from Nutrition.gov
http://www.nutrition.gov

Visit the left-hand column links to Shopping, Cooking, and Meal Planning to gain insight into smart practices to improve meal quality and save money. Learn how to plan meals and read food labels. Learn about cooking methods and recipes, and how to save money by purchasing ingredients after you plan your menu.

eHow: How to Learn to Cook
http://www.ehow.com/how_2166655_learn-to-cook.html

With clear instructions, videos, and other online tools, this website provides a solid introduction to cooking and following recipes.

Meals Matter
http://www.mealsmatter.org

Developed by the Dairy Council of California, this website offers healthy meal planning resources, including information on nutrition, recipes, meal suggestions, quick meal tips, and much more.

Ingredients
Smart Nutrition 101 from the U.S. Department of Agriculture
http://www.nutrition.gov

Click on Smart Nutrition 101 in the left column, and learn about the food pyramid and dietary guidelines to improve your nutrition and health. Understanding the principles of nutrition is the first step to learning to cook and plan healthy meals.

Buying Local
http://www.foodroutes.org/howtobuylocal.jsp

There are many advantages to purchasing local ingredients. Food tends to be fresher, sometimes cheaper, and your purchases help support local farms and suppliers, which is good for the economy.

Find a Farmers' Market
http://apps.ams.usda.gov/FarmersMarkets/

Use this handy search engine developed by the U.S. Department of Agriculture to find local area farmers' markets. Just enter your state and county.

Chapter 19

What to Know About Cholesterol and High Blood Pressure

You went to the doctor for a checkup and found out that your cholesterol is too high. What does this mean? What can you do about it?

Goals:

1) Learn about the risks of high cholesterol, high blood pressure, and heart disease.
2) Learn what you can do to keep your cholesterol and blood pressure at healthy levels.

Use Chapter 51 of Starting Out!®, the resources in this chapter, and your own Internet research to complete the following.

Cholesterol is a naturally occurring substance which the body can either produce itself or get through food. Name two types of food that contain high levels of cholesterol.

1) _____

2) _____

It is important for the body to have some cholesterol for healthy functioning. What are two things the body needs cholesterol for?

1) _____

2) _____

All too often today, people get more cholesterol than the body needs. When this happens, cholesterol circulates in the blood and can start to build up on the artery walls which lead to the heart. What can happen if there is too much cholesterol build-up in the arteries?

_____

_____

_____

You've had your blood pressure taken at the doctor's office before and have heard people say that high blood pressure is bad. What is blood pressure a measure of, anyway?

_____

_____

What causes high blood pressure?

_____

_____

How is high blood pressure connected to heart disease?

_____

_____

Certain common unhealthy activities, known as risk factors, increase your chances of developing heart disease. Name three risk factors for heart disease.

1) _____

2) _____

3) _____

Not all cholesterol is bad. Name the three types of cholesterol, in order from good to bad.

1) _____

2) _____

3) _____

How does good cholesterol reduce the effects of bad cholesterol?

_____

_____

_____

Certain lifestyle habits can help you maintain healthy cholesterol levels. What are some common foods that can lower your cholesterol levels?

_____

_____

_____

What are some other things you can do to lower your cholesterol, and also lower your risk of heart disease?

_____

_____

_____

_____

 **Resources**

Cholesterol
MedlinePlus: Cholesterol
http://www.nlm.nih.gov/medlineplus/cholesterol.html

A variety of resources on cholesterol can be found at Medlineplus, the federal government's online medical reference system. Read the overview sites, and then learn something about research on cholesterol as well as screening and prevention.

National Cholesterol Education Program
http://www.nhlbi.nih.gov/chd/

Live Healthier, Live Longer. That is the goal promoted by the National Cholesterol Education Program, which is described on this government website. Learn about preventing heart disease and high cholesterol through information that relates to young people as well as the older population.

National Heart, Lung, and Blood Institute: High Blood Cholesterol
http://www.nhlbi.nih.gov/health/dci/Diseases/Hbc/HBC_WhatIs.html

Learn about high cholesterol, including signs, symptoms, diagnosis, and treatments at this website of one of the agencies of the National Institutes of Health.

Heart Disease
Heart Disease at the Centers for Disease Control and Prevention
http://www.cdc.gov/heartdisease

Heart disease is the leading cause of death in the United States and is a major cause of disability. Visit this website to learn about heart disease and how you can prevent it.

MayoClinic.com: Heart Disease
http://www.mayoclinic.com/health/heart-disease/HB99999

One of the foremost medical centers in America, the Mayo Clinic offers comprehensive information about heart disease, including screening, diagnosis, risk factors, and prevention.

American Heart Association
http://www.americanheart.org

Learn about warning signs of heart disease, and explore information on dozens of different heart conditions.

Chapter 20

Exercise and Physical Fitness: Choosing a Program that Works

Now that you have a plan to improve your diet, it's time to think about getting more exercise. Where should you begin? Are competitive sports and the gym the only options? What kinds of activities are considered exercise?

✓ Check all that are forms of exercise.

- [ ] Taking the stairs instead of the elevator
- [ ] Running on a treadmill, track, or trail
- [ ] Walking your dog
- [ ] Aerobics class
- [ ] Biking to the store
- [ ] Sweeping, vacuuming, or mopping the floor
- [ ] Mowing the lawn
- [ ] Dancing

Goals:

1) Learn about the health benefits of exercise.
2) Think of ways to incorporate different types of activities into an active lifestyle.

Use Part XII of Starting Out!® and your own Internet research to complete the following.

Though nutrition is very important, the other key to staying healthy is making physical fitness part of your life. List three health benefits of exercise:

1) _____

2) _____

3) _____

Conversely, being overweight or obese puts a greater strain on the body, and can lead to a number of diseases and health conditions. List three here:

1) _____

2) _____

3) _____

The good thing about exercise is that there are so many different activities you can do, that everyone is sure to find something suitable. Even some common household activities can give you a moderate or low-impact work-out. Give two examples of these kinds of activities (not previously listed):

1) _____

2) _____

It's important to vary low-impact activity with more vigorous exercise. Sports are what people most often think of, but there are also many non-competitive activities you can do on your own or with friends. Are there any types of high impact activity that you already engage in?

_____
_____

What are two new activities that you'd like to try?

_____
_____

Now it's time to set some goals! As you have learned, physical fitness is an important part of a healthy life, and can be easy and fun to include in your daily routine. However, it is helpful to make a plan to make sure you meet the recommended amount of weekly exercise. First, determine your Body Mass Index, or BMI. This is a way to judge general fitness by comparing height, weight, and sometimes frame structure. Look online and find out your BMI. The Centers for Disease Control and Prevention provides a BMI calculator at *http://www.cdc.gov/ healthyweight/assessing/bmi/adult_bmi/english_bmi_calculator/bmi_calculator.html*.

Cardiovascular exercises build your heart and lungs' endurance, while strength-building and resistance activities increase your muscle strength. Scientists recommend at least 30 minutes of moderate exercise on most days, or at least 20 minutes of vigorous exercise three days a week. Strength training is recommended two days per week.

Name two types of moderate exercise you can incorporate into your weekly routine.

1) _____

2) _____

Name one vigorous exercise you can incorporate into your weekly routine.

_____

Name one strength-training activity you can incorporate into your weekly routine.

_____

In addition, set a long-term goal of increasing, decreasing, or maintaining your weight:

_____
_____
_____
_____

Resources

The President's Council on Physical Fitness and Sports
http://www.fitness.gov/

The Council offers the 2008 Physical Activity Guidelines for Americans, along with Physical Activity Guides for individuals seeking to improve their health and well-being. Both of these resources can be downloaded.

Medlineplus: Exercise and Physical Fitness
http://www.nlm.nih.gov/medlineplus/exerciseandphysicalfitness.html

Extensive resources from many reliable sources can be found at this site from Medlineplus, a government health information website. There are numerous articles on topics related to exercise and fitness, including many recommended fitness programs.

HealthierUS.gov: Fitness, Health, and Wellness
http://www.healthierus.gov/

The HealthierUS initiative is a national effort to improve people's lives, prevent and reduce the costs of disease, and promote community health and wellness.

Chapter 21

Getting Help When You're Feeling Sick

Y ou wake up one morning with a fever, headache, and muscle aches; you're feeling really sick. Your regular doctor is back in your hometown, and you don't know who to go see. You saw some kind of clinic down the street; would it be okay to go there? How do you pay for your visit? Is this illness worth a trip to the doctor anyway?

Goals:

1) Learn what symptoms should not be ignored.
2) Learn about college and university student insurance plans and employer-based group insurance programs.
3) Learn about getting insurance, if you don't have any.
4) Learn about different types of medical providers.

Use Part XIII of Starting Out!®, the resources in this chapter, and your own Internet research to respond to the following:

We've all had colds before — stuffed noses, fatigue, slight cough. Colds will generally get better on their own with rest. When is it time to go to the doctor?

✓ Which of the following symptoms shouldn't be ignored?

☐	Persistent abdominal pain	☐	An atypical (for you) headache
☐	Memory loss	☐	Vertigo, weakness, or loss of coordination
☐	Trouble breathing	☐	Persistent or spreading itchy rash
☐	Weight loss without trying to lose weight; unexplained weight loss		

In this scenario, you currently don't have insurance. But do you need insurance? If you are a generally healthy person, your typical yearly health care costs will probably be pretty low. But what if you become ill or injured? How much does an average doctor's visit cost? Look online, search "cost uninsured doctor visit," and find two quotes:

1) _____

2) _____

You are likely to pay even more for a hospital stay. So you need to make a choice. You can pay these costs out-of-pocket, perhaps starting a special bank account to save money just for medical expenses. You can also look into getting insurance. To begin, use the resources in this chapter to define some typical insurance terms:

Health Maintenance Organization (HMO):
Health Savings Account (HSA):
Primary Care Provider/Physician:
Basic Benefits:
Deductible:
Out-of-Pocket Limit:
Lifetime Maximum:
Copayment:
Claim:
Pre-existing conditions:

When determining what type of insurance to get, decide what type of deductible is best for you and what type of coverage you need. Also, is insurance available through your school or an employer-based group program? This is usually the most affordable way to get health insurance.

If you cannot get insurance through your employer or school, then you need to contact companies to find out what your options are for an individual plan. Either way, you will probably be given the option of choosing between several plans. Check out the chart on the next page and answer the questions that follow it.

Plan Name	Health Insurance for You	Wellness Healthcare	Health Solutions
Monthly Payment	$437.93	$785.13	$654.75
Deductible	$2,500	$500	$1000
Coinsurance/ Copayment	You pay 10% after deductible is met	$25 copayment	You pay 90% until deductible is met, $10 after deductible
Provider	May use any healthcare provider	Must use Primary Care Provider (PCP), or physician referred by PCP	May use any in-network provider
Prescription Plan	100% coverage after the deductible is met	You pay a $20 copayment after deductible is met	$20 copayment
Emergency Care	100% coverage after the deductible is met	$50 copayment if not admitted to hospital	$75 copayment if not admitted to hospital

With all above plans, can you go to any doctor you want? If not, how are you limited?

_____

_____

Which plans require you to pay full price for your medicine, until the deductible is met?

_____

_____

If you go to the emergency room, but are not admitted to the hospital, how much will you pay under the Health Insurance for You plan?

_____

How much would you pay for a $100 doctor's visit under each of these plans?

_____

_____

Which of the above three plans would you choose? Why?

_____

_____

You will likely visit your primary care provider for most of your medical needs. But in some cases, you might not be able to get to your primary care provider. You might be away from home, or you might get sick after the provider's hours. In these or other situations, you can't wait to make a regular appointment. What are your options? In most cases, you can go to a local hospital's emergency room or an urgent care clinic. Also, community health clinics frequently offer extended hours and affordable prices.

It's good to know ahead of time what your options are. Please list one hospital as well as an urgent care center or a community health clinic close to your home:

	Name	Location and Phone Number
Hospital		
After-Hours Clinic		

When going to an emergency facility or to your primary provider for the first time, it is helpful to bring records of your medical conditions, recent tests, current medications, and more. Do you know the following about your medical history?

Health insurance provider, if any:

_____

Allergies, if any:

_____

_____

Immunizations and dates:

_____

_____

_____

Medications, vitamins, and/or supplements you are taking:

_____

_____

Blood type:

_____

Previous illnesses:

_____

_____

_____

Resources

Health Insurance

US Department of Labor: Consumer Information on Health Plans

http://www.dol.gov/dol/topic/health-plans/consumerinfhealth.htm

This page contains numerous links to information on health and benefit plans. Topics include continuation of health coverage (COBRA), mental health benefits, plan information, participant rights, and much more.

Questions and Answers About Health Insurance

http://www.ahrq.gov/consumer/insuranceqa/index.html#Contents

The federal Agency for Healthcare Research and Quality offers a useful question and answer format to explore aspects of health insurance, including terms, types of plans, the importance of health insurance, and how to secure health insurance.

Finding a Physician

DoctorFinder from the American Medical Association

http://www.ama-assn.org

DoctorFinder provides you with basic professional information on virtually every licensed physician in the United States. This includes more than 814,000 doctors. Select "DoctorFinder" from the "Jump to" menu.

MedlinePlus: Choosing a Doctor or Healthcare Service

http://www.nlm.nih.gov/medlineplus/choosingadoctororhealthcareservice.html

Many useful articles offer sound advice about selecting a physician for you, your family, or for individuals with special needs. The information comes from reliable professional medical organizations and government agencies.

MedlinePlus: Directories

http://www.nlm.nih.gov/medlineplus/directories.html

This site can help you locate more than just doctors. Follow one of the many links to find dentists, clinics, hospitals, nutritionists, and massage therapists. There are also links to a variety of specialists.

Walk-in Clinics and Emergency Services

Finding an Urgent Care Center

http://secure.ucaoa.org/ucaoa_orgs.php

The Urgent Care Association of America offers a useful search engine to locate a walk-in clinic or an urgent care center in your community.

Before Going to the Emergency Room

http://www.thehealthpages.com/articles/ar-erinf.html

This general health information website offers useful information about when to and when not to go to an emergency room, how emergency rooms work, information to bring with you, and other recommendations.

Chapter 22

Learning About Mental Health Issues

A friend seems really down and unhappy but can't explain specifically why. This friend has had ups and downs before, but not like this. Nothing seems to help him feel better. What's wrong? What can you do?

Goals:

1) Recognize different symptoms of depression.
2) Learn about ways depression can be treated and what can happen if it is not treated.
3) Learn how to find out about other mental health concerns.

Use Chapters 55 and 61 of Starting Out!®, the resources in this chapter, and your own Internet research to complete the following.

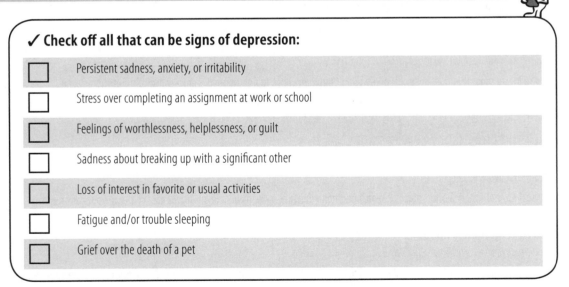

✓ **Check off all that can be signs of depression:**

☐ Persistent sadness, anxiety, or irritability

☐ Stress over completing an assignment at work or school

☐ Feelings of worthlessness, helplessness, or guilt

☐ Sadness about breaking up with a significant other

☐ Loss of interest in favorite or usual activities

☐ Fatigue and/or trouble sleeping

☐ Grief over the death of a pet

All of us have felt sad before. Shouldn't your friend be able to snap out of it? Why is clinical depression different from a short-term case of the "blues?" (hint: look for information on depression and the brain)

_____

_____

_____

If not addressed, depression can have serious consequences. What are some of the effects depression can have on a person's life?

_____

_____

If a friend or family member suffers from depression, what can you do? Where could someone get help?

_____

_____

Depression is not the only mental health challenge people can face. Write a brief description of the following common disorders:

Alcoholism:

_____

_____

Attention-Deficit Hyperactivity Disorder:

_____

_____

Anorexia Nervosa:

_____

_____

Nicotine Dependence:

_____

_____

Post-Traumatic Stress Disorder:

_____

_____

 **Resources**

National Institute of Mental Health: Mental Health Topics

http://www.nimh.nih.gov/health/topics/index.shtml

The NIMH provides extensive information on more than a dozen common mental health conditions, such as depression, bipolar disorder, and anxiety disorders. There are also research papers, statistics, and mental health data relative to men, women, children, and older individuals.

National Mental Health Information Center

http://mentalhealth.samhsa.gov/

The Substance Abuse and Mental Health Services Administration (SAMHSA), a federal agency, provides valuable information on mental health, suicide prevention, youth violence prevention, and other topics of interest. There are also articles and papers on current topics, national mental health hotlines, and a general call center to seek advice.

Medline Plus: Mental Health and Behavior

http://www.nlm.nih.gov/medlineplus/mentalhealthandbehavior.html

Medlineplus is a federal database, organized alphabetically, on hundreds of medical topics, including mental health and behavioral issues. Each topical link leads to extensive articles, current news, and medical information.

Mental Health America

http://www.nmha.org/index.cfm

This leading mental health non-profit organization offers in-depth information by audience, disorder, and treatment for numerous mental health conditions and issues, covering such areas as anxiety disorders, eating disorders, grief, stress, substance abuse, suicide, trauma, and military-related mental health problems.

Chapter 23

Party Pressure, Street Drugs, and Unplanned Consequences

Despite the great reviews from some of the other party-goers, you know you've heard that there can be negative effects from different drugs, and some can even be life-threatening in the wrong dose. What should you do?

Goals:

1) Learn about the dangers of different drugs, as well as alcohol and tobacco.
2) Learn about the dangers of club drugs and how to avoid taking drugs without your knowledge.
3) Learn about the legal consequences of drug use.
4) Learn how to get help for drug addiction.
5) Learn how to defend yourself against peer pressure.

Use Part XIV of Starting Out!®, the resources in this chapter, and your own Internet research to complete the following.

There are many different types of drugs, which have a range of effects on your body. Fill in the following chart about the short- and long-term effects of drug abuse. A short-term effect could be dizziness or excess energy; a long-term effect could be damaged mental faculties or lung cancer.

Drug Name	Street Name	Short Term Effects	Long Term Effects
Alcohol			
Tobacco			
Steroids			

Amphetamines			
Club Drugs			
Cocaine			
Marijuana			
Oxycontin (a pre-scription drug)			
Inhalants			

The group of drugs called "Club Drugs" has another concern associated with it: these drugs can be slipped into drinks and cause the victim to lose consciousness or become immobilized and then assaulted. What are some ways to protect yourself from taking drugs without your knowledge?

1) _____

2) _____

In addition to health and social consequences of drug use, there will be legal ramifications if you are caught using, possessing, or selling illegal drugs. Pick out an illegal drug from the table above and find out what will happen in your state if you are found in possession of that drug.

_____
_____

Imagine that a friend of yours has become addicted to drugs, alcohol, or inhalants. Find a rehabilitation resource in your state that you could recommend.

_____
_____

What else could you do to help your friend?

_____
_____
_____

The best thing for you to do if you are offered drugs is to stand up to peer pressure and just say no. But it isn't always easy! What are some things you can do to overcome peer pressure?

_____
_____

 **Resources**

Substance Abuse and Club Drugs
Medline Plus: Drug Abuse
http://www.nlm.nih.gov/medlineplus/drugabuse.html

A comprehensive resource on drug abuse is available at Medlineplus, the consumer reference site of the National Library of Medicine. Learn about the properties and risks of club drugs and alcohol, as well as treatment and prevention programs.

The Truth About Club Drugs
http://ncadi.samhsa.gov/govpubs/phd852/

The government's National Clearinghouse on Alcohol and Drug Information is part of the Substance Abuse and Mental Health Services Administration (SAMHSA). This site offers reliable information on the risks and detrimental effects of club drugs on the brain, motor control, vision, and balance.

Penalties
U.S. Drug Enforcement Administration: Federal Trafficking Penalties
http://www.usdoj.gov/dea/agency/penalties.htm

A chart showing the penalties for trafficking in drugs is presented at this government website of the Drug Enforcement Administration, an agency of the Department of Justice.

Rehabilitation
Substance Abuse Treatment Facility Locator
http://dasis3.samhsa.gov/

The Substance Abuse and Mental Health Services Administration of the federal government presents a map and accompanying search engine for individuals to locate treatment programs for substance abuse in every state.

Peer Pressure
Peer Pressure
http://www.thecoolspot.gov/pressures.asp

Directed at teens and young adults, this government website explains the power of peer pressure, which can lure individuals into alcohol and drug use, as well as other activities that may present personal risks.

Chapter 24

Elections, Voting, and Political Awareness

An election is coming up, and you've never voted before. You've watched a lot of television commercials about the different candidates, but you still don't know who to choose for the different offices. How do you find more information on the candidates? Where do you go to vote?

Goals:

1) Learn about voting rights.
2) Learn how to register to vote. Learn how to register with a party, or as an independent.
3) Learn how to research national, state, and local candidates.
4) Learn how to participate further, either by volunteering for a campaign or polling station or running for office yourself.

Use Chapter 66 of Starting Out!®, the resources in this chapter, and your own Internet research to complete the following.

In the United States, any U.S. citizen 18 and above has the right to vote. But first, you need to register. Look up how to register to vote in your state and town.

Is there a deadline for registering?	
What ID do you need to bring with you when you register to vote?	
Find the location of your polling place:	
What are your polling place hours?	

What can you do if you will be out of town on Election Day? Can you still vote?

_____

_____

Before you vote, you should learn more about the candidates and the issues. Who are your U.S. Senators? What are the URLs of their websites?

Name	Website
U.S. Senator 1:	
U.S. Senator 2:	

What is the name of your state senator and district representative?

State Senator: _____

District Representative: _____

Who is the mayor or government head in your city or town?

_____

People often base their votes on issues that are important to them. What public issues concern you the most?

_____

_____

_____

You may find that you want to be more involved in politics and elections. One option is to volunteer on Election Day. You might also consider volunteering for a political party or for a particular candidate. It is very easy to sign up, and there are lots of things you can do to help, from putting a sign in your yard, to making phone calls, to going door-to-door. Do any of these activities interest you?

_____

_____

If you become very passionate about politics, you may want to consider running for office at some point. There are many opportunities including serving on town councils and committees, boards of education, and even running for mayor! If you were to run for office or serve on a municipal committee, what issues might interest you most?

_____

_____

_____

 **Resources**

Voting
Can I Vote?

http://www.canivote.org

Figure out how and where to vote by using this convenient website that has a huge national database of voting places.

Federal Voting Assistance Program

http://www.fvap.gov/

For U.S. citizens living outside of the country, this government website provides essential information on how to vote from abroad.

Candidates and Election Information
Vote 411: Election Information You Need

http://www.vote411.org/

Learn about voting, registering, political candidates, polling places, and ballot issues at this comprehensive website.

Fact Check

http://www.factcheck.org/

This non-partisan website will enable visitors to check facts and claims they may read about to see if they are correct. By verifying information, this project helps hold candidates and politicians responsible for their statements.

Running for Office
RunForOffice.org

http://www.runforoffice.org/

If you think you might like to hold public office, whether in a small town or on the national scene, this website is a good starting place to learn whether you have the qualifications.

Chapter 25

All About Jury Duty: A Compulsory Citizen Responsibility

Y ou have been called for jury duty while you are recuperating from your broken leg. What is jury duty? Are you required to serve? What about your job?

Goals:

1) Learn what jury duty entails.
2) Learn about the obligations of jury duty.
3) Learn about the requirements of serving as a juror.

Use Chapter 67 of Starting Out!®, the resources in this chapter, and your own Internet research to complete the following.

What is a juror? Why do we have juries in the United States?

_____
_____
_____

How are jurors selected?

_____
_____
_____

List three qualifications of a juror.

1) _____

2) _____

3) _____

What may disqualify you from being a juror? Give two examples:

1) _____

2) _____

What happens to your job during jury duty?

_____

_____

_____

Do you receive any compensation for being a juror?

_____

_____

How long does jury duty last?

_____

_____

Can jury duty be postponed?

_____

Is jury duty mandatory?

_____

 **Resources**

Fully Informed Jury Association

http://www.fija.org/

Access the Juror's Guide to learn about juries and jury duties. Learn about grand juries and petit juries. Learn what to do when you are called for jury duty. There is also a video that explains jury duty.

National Center for State Courts

http://www.ncsconline.org/

The National Center for State Courts provides a search engine where visitors can access information on the court system of any state. Just click on "Browse by State" to access a clickable map to find details about court systems of individual states.

Chapter 26

Opportunities and Options in Military Service

You just got a phone call from the local navy recruiter. You've heard that serving in the navy has educational and job training benefits. But it would probably mean leaving home at some point to serve overseas. You think you might like to serve our country, but would you have to be in combat? Is this the right choice for you?

Goals:

1) Learn about the educational benefits of serving in the military.
2) Learn about the job training benefits of and career opportunities in military service.
3) Learn about the personal growth gained from military service.

Use Chapters 70 and 71 of Starting Out!®, the resources in this chapter, and your own Internet research to complete the following.

What exactly are the central differences between the branches of the military? Some might seem obvious, like the navy and the air force, but the difference between the army and the marines might sound a little more subtle. Summarize in one or two sentences the mission and duties of the different branches.

Air Force:	
Army:	
Coast Guard:	
Marine Corps:	
Navy:	

Military service might not be right for you. But if it is, there are many benefits to serving. If you are undecided, you may find military service to be a better opportunity than you thought.

First, there are educational benefits from serving in the military. List some of these benefits here:

_____
_____
_____

You can also receive educational benefits as a veteran. Use the websites listed in the Resources section to find state-by-state educational benefits for veterans, that is, people who have completed their military service. Locate the information for your state.

What benefits are offered?

_____

What are the terms of the financial aid?

_____
_____

These days, if you decide you'd like to go into the service, you don't just become a soldier. There are actually many job options available, and the training you receive in the military can be applied to a civilian career. Military.com recommends choosing three jobs when getting ready to enlist. Visit *http://www.military.com/recruiting* and select "Step 6: Get the best job." Then choose a branch and pick three potential occupations within that branch. Try the "Interest Matcher" if you can't decide.

Branch:

Job 1: _____

Job 2: _____

Job 3: _____

The minimum enlistment time is eight years, whether it is spent on active duty or in the reserves. Some people choose to make the military a lifetime career. There are three potential paths: enlisted personnel, warrant officer, or commissioned officer. In terms of education, officers usually require at least a bachelor's degree, while enlisted personnel typically need to have a high school diploma or GED. While each path offers different careers, each allows opportunities for advancement. Select a branch of the military and either officer (O) or enlisted personnel (EP) level:

Branch: _____

Level: _____

Now, with the help of the *Occupational Outlook Handbook* (*www.bls.gov/oco/ocos249.htm*), fill in the following chart:

Grade:	
Title/Rank:	
Monthly pay after 4 years of service:	
Monthly pay after 12 years of service:	

Becoming a member of the military means a life shaped by discipline, service, and ethics, and therefore is an opportunity for personal growth. What are some of the personal benefits, unrelated to education and careers, of military service?

1) _____

2) _____

In terms of ethics and values, each branch of the military has its own set of core values, which the members live by and use as a guide to life and service. List the core values for one branch of the United State Military:

Branch: _____

Values: _____

 **Resources**

Service, Education, and Benefits
Department of Defense Directory of Programs
http://www.defenselink.mil/sites/

By visiting this directory, you can select and visit the appropriate website covering aspects of our country's defense operations. Along with links to each branch of the military services, there are dozens of other useful links covering deployment, civilian job opportunities, the National Guard and Reserve, pay levels, and recruiting.

Reserve Officers' Training Corps (ROTC)
http://www.military.com/rotc

ROTC programs were designed to augment the service academies in producing leaders and managers for the armed forces. The Army, Navy, Marine Corps, and Air Force offer ROTC scholarships to eligible students, as explained at this website.

Military Service Academies
http://www.defenselink.mil/faq/pis/20.html

This Department of Defense website gives the contact addresses for each of the branches of the armed services. You can click on any name and follow the link to a full website about that service branch. Here you will learn about the U.S. Military Academy, the Naval Academy, the Air Force Academy, the Coast Guard Academy, and the Merchant Marine Academy.

Military Benefits
http://www.militarybenefits.com/

This comprehensive website provides information on military benefits, covering those in active duty as well as veterans. Benefits relate to education and scholarships, financial and family assistance, job training and career development, employment assistance, and many other important topics.

Careers
Department of Defense: ASVAB Program
http://www.asvabprogram.com/

Offering useful information for different age groups concerning career development, the ASVAB Program administered by the Department of Defense is an excellent starting point to begin a career path exploration.

Occupational Outlook Handbook: Job Opportunities in the Armed Forces
http://www.bls.gov/OCO/ocos249.htm

This Bureau of Labor Statistics website has extensive information on jobs in the armed forces. You can also move from this page to any part of the database to explore careers, skill sets, training requirements, financial aid, and other related topics.

Today's Military: Careers
http://www.todaysmilitary.com/careers

Explore dozens of interesting career possibilities with the Armed Forces at this user-friendly website. The site has a lengthy alphabetical list of service occupations, along with resources on education and benefits.

Personal Growth and Values
GoArmy.com: Personal Growth and Values
http://www.goarmy.com/life/living_the_army_values.jsp

Learn about the enduring values of the army, and how they will impact your entire life if you join this branch.

Navy.com: Personal Development
http://www.navy.com/about/during/personaldevelopment/

Military service centers around honor, courage, and commitment. Visit this website to understand how the U.S. Navy can help you develop these values.

Core Values of the United States Air Force

http://www.airforce.com/learn-about/our-values

Just as the other services have their own traditions and values, so does the U.S. Air Force. Learn about these values on this site.

Marines: Core Values

http://officer2.marines.com/marine/quality_citizens/core_values

Learn about the traditions and values of service in the Marine Corps through this website, which also includes information on professional development, becoming an officer, and leadership skills.

Coast Guard: Leaders

http://www.uscg.mil/top/leaders.asp

Explore the Coast Guard's core values, leadership standards, and professionalism. Read about how service in the Coast Guard can be a rewarding career.

Chapter 27

The President Announces a Code Orange Alert

You were watching the news this morning when the President announced that the country is in a code orange alert. What does that mean? Is this an emergency? What should you do?

Goals:

1) Learn about homeland security.
2) Learn about emergency preparedness.

Use Chapter 73 of Starting Out!®, the resources in this chapter, and your own Internet research to complete the following.

Emergencies can come from man-made causes or natural ones. An example of a natural disaster would be an earthquake or tornado. A man-made emergency could be an explosion or a blackout.

The Department of Homeland Security (DHS) has a five-level, color-coded advisory system. What do the different levels mean? What are some recommended preparedness steps you should take for each level?

Color	Green	Blue	Yellow	Orange	Red
Level of Risk					
Recommended Step #1					
Recommended Step #2					

How does the DHS determine the daily security level?

_____

_____

Each region of the country is susceptible to different emergencies from certain natural or man-made disasters. Name two potential disasters for your area, using Ready.gov's "Be Informed" page. What can you do to prepare for them?

	Disaster:	Preparation:
1		
2		

What are some of the resources in your state that can help you deal with emergencies?

_____

_____

_____

Ready.gov suggests preparing an emergency preparedness kit, so that you'll have the basics for survival in case of an emergency. List four things that are recommended for your kit:

1) _____

2) _____

3) _____

4) _____

Are you and your family prepared for an emergency? Test your Readiness Quotient at *http://www.whatsyourrq. org*, and write down your score.

_____

_____

Resources

U.S. Department of Homeland Security

http://www.dhs.gov/index.shtm

Extensive resources on the topic of homeland security can be found at the agency's website, including information sharing, prevention, preparedness and response, news, and the threat-level system.

Are You Ready? Guide

http://www.fema.gov/areyouready/index.shtm

Learn about the different threat conditions and what they mean, as well as how to prepare and conduct yourself in case of emergency.

Ready.gov

http://www.ready.gov

Learn how to prepare, plan, and stay informed at the federal government's citizen readiness website.

What's Your Readiness Quotient?

http://www.whatsyourrq.org/

Are you ready for an emergency? Do you know what to do and where to go? Take this simple online test to determine your level of readiness in case of a national or local disaster.

Chapter 28

Getting Ready for an Overseas Trip: What You Need to Know

You've been saving up money for a special vacation, and now you're going to travel overseas! You know you need to get a passport, but you don't know where to get one. Are there any other documents you need? What else should you know about traveling abroad?

Goals:

1) Learn about passports and customs.
2) Learn about consular assistance.
3) Learn about foreign travel risks.
4) Learn about studying and working abroad.

Use Chapter 68 and Part XVIII of Starting Out!®, the resources in this chapter, and your own Internet research to complete the following.

If you are getting your passport for the first time, you need to go in person to one of the many passport acceptance facilities throughout the country. Go to the Passport Acceptance Facility Search Page at *http://iafdb.travel.state.gov* and locate two passport acceptance facilities near you:

1) _____

2) _____

What are the three items you need to bring with you when applying?

1) _____

2) _____

3) _____

Each country is unique, and has traditions, laws, safety concerns, and other rules and issues that prepared travelers should be aware of and respect. Choose a country you would like to visit, and answer the following questions.

Country: _____

What are the entry requirements?

_____
_____
_____

Are special vaccinations required or suggested?

_____
_____

Where is the nearest United States Embassy or Consulate?

_____

Does this country have any particular personal safety or crime concerns?

_____
_____

Are there any special circumstances to be aware of?

_____
_____
_____

The U.S. Government issues travel warnings for entire countries when there are long term conditions that make that country dangerous or unstable. Travel alerts concern short term conditions that increase risk to U.S. citizens, such as natural disasters or high-profile events. Locate the Travel Warnings section of *http://www.travel. state.gov* and write down a country for which a travel warning has been issued:

_____

If you run into a problem while you are overseas, your U.S. Embassy or Consulate may be able to help you. Name two ways in which an Embassy or Consulate can help you while you're in a foreign country.

    1) _____

    2) _____

When you return to the United States, you will pass through Customs. There are certain items that may not be brought into the United States, and it is the duty of Customs to make sure these items do not enter the country. What are three common items you cannot bring into the United States from a foreign country?

    1) _____

    2) _____

    3) _____

You may decide that you'd like to spend a longer amount of time in a foreign country. You can arrange for extended stays through school or through a job or volunteer program. There are many study abroad programs; some are sponsored by American universities, while others are sponsored directly through a foreign school. Use one of the study abroad websites in the resources section to locate a study abroad program.

Country:

_____

School:

_____

Program of study:

_____

There are many opportunities for someone interested in working or volunteering abroad. One of them is the Peace Corps, a U.S. government program. Other options include working for an embassy or a U.S. company which has offices abroad. Teaching English as a foreign language is also a popular option.

Is it better to have a job arranged before you leave home? Explain.

_____
_____
_____
_____

 **Resources**

Travel
State Department Bureau of Consular Affairs: Travel Resources
http://www.travel.state.gov

If you are considering a trip abroad, this website from the U.S. State Department provides travel advisories, including medical alerts; passport and visa information; contact information for emergency assistance abroad; and other important topics for travelers.

Websites of U.S. Embassies, Consulates, and Diplomatic Missions
http://www.usembassy.gov/

The State Department network of foreign embassies and consulates can be a very important resource when you are in an unfamiliar country and run into problems or need immediate assistance.

Study

U.S. State Department: Students Abroad

http://studentsabroad.state.gov

If you have plans to study abroad, visit this State Department website to learn about travel documents, health issues, emergencies, smart travel, cultural exchanges, and much more.

StudyAbroad.com: Programs and Opportunities

http://www.studyabroad.com

One of the largest websites on foreign study opportunities and information, StudyAbroad is an excellent place to learn about specific programs, internships, volunteering, language programs, scholarships, and financial aid.

Volunteering

Peace Corps

http://www.peacecorps.gov/index.cfm

President John F. Kennedy challenged students in the 1960s to volunteer their time to help the less fortunate in foreign countries. From a small beginning, this international program has grown and offered thousands of people, young and old, the chance to offer their skills and time to communities across the globe.

VolunteerAbroad

http://www.volunteerabroad.com

This website offers a useful search engine to locate volunteer programs abroad. There are profiles of foreign opportunities, along with resources on financial aid and scholarships, travel, and other topics.

Working Abroad

Occupational Outlook Quarterly: Working Abroad

http://www.bls.gov/opub/ooq/2006/fall/art01.htm

If you are interested in working abroad, the Occupational Outlook Handbook issued by the U.S. Department of Labor offers information on international internships and entry-level jobs.

InterExchange Foundation

http://www.interexchange.org/

Founded in 2006, this non-profit foundation offers grants to young people to further their cultural awareness through meaningful work experiences abroad.

Chapter 29

Tracking Computer Viruses and Protecting Your Identity

Since you've been back from your vacation, your computer has been really slow, and it keeps crashing. One of your friends thinks your computer has a virus. He asked if you had firewall protection, but you're not sure. What's going on? What can you do?

Goals:

1) Learn about spam. Learn about different viruses and other computer hazards.
2) Find out about firewalls and virus protection.
3) Learn how to protect your personal information while visiting websites.
4) Learn how to be safe on social networking sites.

Use the resources in this chapter and your own Internet research to complete the following.

Everyone likes to get e-mails. But what should you do if you don't recognize the address of the person sending the e-mail?

_____

_____

What is spam? How can it be harmful?

_____

_____

What are spyware and malware? How can they be harmful?

_____

_____

What are cookies? How can they be harmful?

_____

_____

What are the differences between computer viruses, computer worms, and Trojan horses? Why are they harmful?

_____

_____

There are many types of anti-virus products available. What are three features to look for when purchasing one of these programs?

     1) _____

     2) _____

     3) _____

Why is it important that your anti-virus software update itself regularly?

_____

_____

It is important to have a secure password that's not too short and has both letters and numbers. Use passwords that are hard for people to guess. Why is it important to have secure passwords?

_____

What is a hacker?

_____

How can you protect your computer from them?

_____

_____

In the case of a major computer crash, it's important to have backups of your most important information, the information you wouldn't want to lose. Do you back up your files? What are ways to back up files?

_____

How often?

_____

Just because you may be anonymous when you're surfing the web, doesn't mean your computer is. What are the current security settings on your web browser?

_____

Is your computer as safe as it can be?

_____

What are three things you can do to make surfing the Internet more safe?

     1) _____

     2) _____

3) _____

Name two things you can do to protect yourself while shopping online.

1) _____

2) _____

Social networking can be a lot of fun, and it can help you stay connected with friends all over the world. However, if you make yourself too open, you could be putting yourself in danger. Which of the following practices do you follow? **Circle one from each of the following pairs:**

I allow everyone to see my profile.
OR
I only allow people I know and trust to view my information.

I post my e-mail and phone numbers so new friends can have them.
OR
I only allow people I trust to have my contact information, and send it to them privately.

If I've never met my Internet friend in person.
I can count on the information in his or her profile to be accurate.
OR
I can't be sure if his or her profile information is reliable.

 **Resources**

Cyber Security Tips

http://www.us-cert.gov/cas/tips/

This Department of Homeland Security cyber security website offers useful suggestions for computer security. There are short discussions on major security topics, and explanations of technical terms.

Protect Your Computer and Identity Advice from Colorado College

http://helpdesk.coloradocollege.edu/index.php/tips-and-how-to/protect-your-computer/

Colorado College offers a computer security Help Desk at this website to explain computer threats and risks of identity theft. This site can help you acquire the knowledge and tools to protect your computer and gain personal safety as well.

Chapter 30

Volunteering Your Time

You have some spare time and decide to volunteer in your community. You think you might like to clean up playgrounds or work with animals, but you don't know where to get started. How do you find out about volunteer opportunities? What types of opportunities are out there?

Goals:

1) Learn about different types of volunteer opportunities.
2) Learn about the benefits of volunteering, for you and the organization.
3) Determine your volunteer interests.
4) Learn about volunteer opportunities in your area.

Use Part XIX of Starting Out!®, the resources in this chapter, and your own Internet research to complete the following.

There are a wide variety of possible volunteer opportunities. The following is just a small sampling of some of your options. Check off any of the following that sound interesting to you:

☐	Walking dogs at an animal shelter
☐	Cleaning up litter at a park or beach
☐	Providing information for hospital visitors
☐	Creating a walking trail through the woods
☐	Teaching kids how to read
☐	Delivering meals to seniors
☐	Building a house with other volunteers

☐	Registering voters at a polling station
☐	Writing an article about a non-profit event
☐	Leading a walking tour of historic buildings
☐	Monitoring water quality of a local lake
☐	Monitoring inventory at a food pantry
☐	Working as an usher at a local arts center

Which opportunity, from the above list, would you find most interesting?

_____

Name another way in which you can volunteer that's not on the list.

_____

How do non-profits and other organizations benefit from volunteers?

_____

_____

Volunteering is advantageous to you, as well. What are some personal benefits you can gain from volunteering?

_____

_____

Now that you've thought about your interests and the benefits of volunteering, it's time to find something to do! Use the websites listed in the resource section to locate two volunteer opportunities in your area that appeal to you.

1) _____

2) _____

You may be interested in volunteering in another country. Use the resources listed at the end of this chapter to locate two volunteer opportunities abroad.

1) _____

2) _____

Resources

National Volunteering

Volunteer.gov

http://www.volunteer.gov/gov/

Use this government website to locate opportunities to volunteer in every state doing numerous types of activities, including campground host, construction, conservation education, historic preservation, natural resource planning, and fire protection.

Volunteer Match: Find an organization

http://www.volunteermatch.org/search/orgs.jsp

VolunteerMatch helps communities by matching volunteers to worthwhile projects. Committed to civic engagement, this organization offers extensive online services that help both nonprofits and the volunteers they attract. This service welcomes millions of visitors a year and has become the preferred Internet recruiting tool for more than 70,000 organizations.

International Volunteer Programs

Peace Corps

http://www.peacecorps.gov/

Since the 1960s, this important international volunteer organization founded by President John F. Kennedy has brought thousands of people to places around the world to help build schools, roads, waterlines, housing, hospitals, and much more.

International Volunteer Programs Association

http://www.volunteerinternational.org

This organization provides assistance in identifying reliable non-governmental international volunteer projects and internship programs around the globe.

U.S. State Department: Travel and Medical Warnings Overseas

http://travel.state.gov/

Visit the website of the U.S. State Department and research countries where you may want to volunteer. Learn about travel and terrorism alerts, as well as disease and political risks.